Fob, regardant

Fob Couchant

Fob dansant

CATS *ancient & modern*

CATS
ancient & modern

Frederick Cameron Sillar & Ruth Mary Meyler

Studio Vista

V., T., R-R
Amicis Felinis
Per Hunc Librum
Gratias Agimus

Designed by Arthur Lockwood

© F. C. Sillar and Ruth Meyler 1966

Published in 1966 by Studio Vista Limited
Blue Star House, Highgate Hill, London N19

Reprinted 1967

Set and printed in 11 on 12 pt Garamond

Distributed in Canada by General Publishing Co. Ltd
30 Lesmill Road, Don Mills, Toronto, Ontario

Made and printed in Great Britain by
The Garden City Press Limited
Letchworth, Hertfordshire

Plates printed in Holland
by NV Grafische Industrie, Haarlem

Contents

Unattributed poems, translations and articles are by the authors

List of illustrations

Unless otherwise indicated, illustrations are reproduced from photographs taken by the authors

Acknowledgments

Among the many people who have helped us in the compilation of *Cats Ancient & Modern* we should like to record our special thanks to Lady Aberconway for allowing us to quote from her *A Dictionary of Cat Lovers*, in particular the translation of 'Pangur Ban' by the late Samuel Courtauld. We also wish to thank Mr B. W. Robinson of the Victoria and Albert Museum for allowing us to quote from his book on Kuniyoshi and to reproduce some of his prints by that artist; to the late Carl Winter, Director of the Fitzwilliam Museum, Cambridge, Mr J. P. Palmer and other members of the staff for helping us to find objects for illustration and enabling us to get or take photographs of them; to members of the staff of the Victoria and Albert Museum and the Bowes Museum, Barnard Castle, who also gave us immense help; to Earl of Romney for permission to print the extract from the Wyat papers; to Miss M. E. Jenkin for her witty translation of Balzac's story of Minette; to Dr W. O. Hassall and Mr R. A. May of the Bodleian Library; and the Burgomaster of Ypres for information regarding the Ypres Cat Festival.

We should also like to record our gratitude to the Deans of Bristol, Exeter, Hereford, Lichfield, Wells and Winchester and to many Rectors or Vicars for allowing us to take photographs in cathedrals and churches for use in this book.

We should like to apologise to anyone whose express permission we have failed to obtain through misadventure or inability to trace their address.

For permission to reprint poems and stories the following acknowledgment is gratefully made: to *The Times* for 'Mourka the Cat' (13 January 1943) and 'Tale of a Holy Cat' (27 April 1963); to Mrs W. B. Yeats and Macmillan & Co. and the Macmillan Co., New York, for 'The Cat and the Moon' from *Collected Poems of W. B. Yeats* by William Butler Yeats. Copyright The Macmillan Co. 1919, renewed 1946 by Bertha Georgie Yeats; to the Literary Trustees of Walter de la Mare and the Society of Authors as their representative for 'Five Eyes'; to the Rodale Press, Pennsylvania, for extracts from *Poor Minette* by P.-J. Stahl, translated by Julian Jacobs; to Mr Sandy Wilson and Max Parrish and Co. for extracts from *This is Sylvia*; to Miss Jacquetta Hawkes for her fable *The City of the Cats* published by the Cresset Press Ltd., reprinted by permission of A. D. Peters and Co.; to Macmillan & Co. and the Viking Press for 'The Prayer of the Cat' from *Prayers from the Ark* by Carmen Bernos de Gasztold, translated by Rumer Godden; to the *Observer* for 'The Convert' by Paul Jennings; to the Bodley Head for 'Tobermory' from *The Bodley Head Saki* and to the Viking Press; to Sir Alexander Gray for 'On a cat, ageing'; to the trustees of the Hardy Estate and Macmillan & Co. for 'Last words to a dumb friend' from *The Collected Poems of Thomas Hardy*.

Acknowledgment is gratefully made for permission to reproduce illustrations as indicated in the List of illustrations on pages 9ff.

The harmless necessary cat

From the earliest times, mankind has been fascinated by cats. Artists have been charmed by the grace of the animal, writers and poets by its independence and originality; yet never was there a creature which so divided the human race into two camps – the admirers and the detractors.

'Cats look down upon us, dogs look up to us, pigs is equal.' The aphorism (although said to have been quoted in the House of Commons against a Minister of Agriculture who was pushing an unpopular pig policy) is manifestly imperfect. Pigs are accepted as Man's equals; their attitude is not in question. But it is the attitude of dogs and cats which is described; yet the question is begged as to whether dogs are inferior and cats are superior. However, assumption of status is often a substitute for status itself and Man, being what he is, is more likely to respond with favour to flattery than to condescension; which is doubtless why there are said to be more dog-lovers than cat-lovers.

Indifference towards cats is rare. One may hate or fear cats with the late Field-Marshal Lord Roberts, who, intrepid soldier though he was, could not enter a room where there was a cat without shuddering; or one may adore cats with the French astronomer Lalande, who tried to introduce a cat into the heavens. 'I love cats, I adore cats,' he wrote, 'and may be forgiven for putting one in the sky, after sixty years of hard work.'

'Some men there are love not a gaping pig,' said Shylock, and went on:

> Some that are mad if they behold a cat;
> And others, when the bagpipe sings i' the nose,
> Cannot contain their urine; for affection,
> Mistress of passion, sways it to the mood
> Of what it likes or loathes. Now, for your answer:
> As there is no firm reason to be render'd
> Why he cannot abide a gaping pig;
> Why he a harmless necessary cat;
> Why he a wailing bagpipe; . . . .

'Harmless' and 'necessary' are both adjectives which suggest that Shakespeare was in favour of cats. When, as in *Macbeth*, he speaks of 'letting "I dare not" wait upon "I would", like the poor cat i' the adage', the word 'poor' suggests sympathy. The proverb was quoted by Taverner in 1539 as: 'The Catte wyll fyshe eate, but she wyl not her feete wette.'

In the other camp is surely Rudyard Kipling. The conclusion, in *The Cat That Walked By Himself*, that 'three out of five proper men' would throw boots and axes at cats, could not have been propounded by a cat lover. The Woman in the story was outraged when the Cat remarked, 'I am the Cat that walks by himself and all places are alike to me', but it is that very independence which extorts a respect given to no other animal except, perhaps, the elephant.

The philosophic detachment of the cat is the quality which, perhaps more than any other, leads the traditional Englishman to prefer dogs. It is also probably the reason why the French were among the first European authors to write appreciatively of cats.

'When I am playing with my cat,' wrote Montaigne, 'who knowes whether she have more sport in dallying with me, than I have in gaming with her?' The only Englishman who might have made a similar speculation about cats would have been Dr Samuel Johnson, who, when he thoughtlessly said he had known cats whom he had liked better than Hodge, the cat then in office, observed that Hodge was 'out of countenance', and said immediately, to soothe hurt feelings, that Hodge was a very fine cat indeed.

Many distinguished writers, both French and English, have written of cats; in such a subject, it is important not to confuse sentiment with sentimentality. The latter quality sometimes appears in modern cat books, but never in French or English writings of earlier centuries. Dr Johnson's friend, Christopher Smart, wrote with exquisite sentiment, albeit with some obscurity, about his cat Jeoffry. Théophile Gautier, a passionate cat-lover, wrote with delightful grace about his cats, as, for instance, in his story of his cat called 'Madame Théophile' and the parrot.

The charm and mystery attaching to cats seem particularly to have captivated French writers. Balzac and Victor Hugo, Pierre Loti and Baudelaire, Zola and Boulmier, have all paid tribute in stories, essays or poems. And there are many others too numerous to mention. Of them all, perhaps, Baudelaire captured most notably the transcendental nature of cats; and, indeed, not only their transcendental quality, for he touched on one characteristic which has more influence than many people allow for – the sweet scent of a cat's fur:

> De sa fourrure blonde et brune
> Sort un parfum si doux, qu'un soir
> J'en fus embaumé, pour l'avoir
> Caressée une fois, rien qu'une.

And how well Balzac understood the brilliance which even the mere mention of a cat could give to a description:

This room is in all its glory at about seven in the morning when Madame Vauquer's cat appears downstairs, a sign that his mistress is on the way. He jumps on the sideboards and sniffs at the plates covering several bowls of milk and purrs his good morning to the world.

The room is the dining-room in Madame Vauquer's famous boarding-house where Le Père Goriot lived. But the French had their cat-haters too. Ronsard writes of the unwelcome cat, as will be seen later; and Rabelais used a species of monster-cats, which he named *Les Chats-Fourrés* to carry much bitter satire on the legal profession. These *Chats-Fourrés* '. . . . *sont bestes moult horribles et espouventables: ils mangent les petits enfans et paissent sus des pierres de marbres . . . . Ils ont le poil de la peau non hors sortant, mais au dedans caché . . . .*' Pantagruel, Panurge and their company find themselves in the course of their travels in the country of *Les Chats-Fourrés* and meet their monstrous 'Archduke', Grippeminaud, so called because his claws are much longer and stronger than those of the ordinary '*minon*' or 'puss' and because he is Ermine. Today, one might translate *Chat-Fourré* as 'shyster' or pettifogging lawyer. Grippeminaud will be met later under his *alias* Raminagrobis, in La Fontaine's fable of the cat-judge.

In considering generally whose *ipsissima verba* on cats should be quoted, the field is so wide that choice is exceedingly difficult. Selection can be invidious. Cat-lovers have their favourite authors and their omission may well cause snorts of disapproval; but an anthology is not an encyclopaedia. If Michael Joseph is not quoted, it does not mean that his cat Charles is forgotten; and if Old Possum's Practical Cats do not appear in the text in these pages, they are, after all, in a book of their own which is readily available. To include all the charming tributes to cats by well-known writers of today and yesterday would require a library.

If one did not like cats one would hardly produce a book about them, but it would be wrong to include only those writings which are laudatory. The cat Raminagrobis described by La Fontaine was a dubious character and one not likely to find favour with, say, Sir Compton Mackenzie or Graham Tomson. But the line must be drawn somewhere and though some anthologists might be tempted by the magnificent writing to include extracts from Edgar Allan Poe's *The Black Cat,* the tale is so horrific in its description of the decadence of the human hero of the story, if such he can be called, that it had better be left where it is in *Tales of Mystery and Imagination* and given no place here. That same Black Cat might be regarded by some enquirers as one of the 'black' cats described by Patricia Dale-Green in her book, *The Cult of the Cat,* but he is not, properly speaking, a witch-cat or a witch's familiar. He is a kind of devil-cat used by the Powers of Light to vanquish those of darkness. He is a super-natural cat rather than a magical cat – a kind of M. R. James cat rather than a monster or wizard cat – which only goes to show the pitfalls of classification.

Some of the best known monster-cat stories come from the East, such as the Japanese tale of Schippeitaro, the brave dog who helps his master to overcome the terrible monster-cat who regularly requires a young maiden for his feast. 'Tell it not to Schippeitaro!' is the unavailing cry of the Monster-Cat's minions.

As a foil to monster-cats, there are beneficent fairy-cats, such as the White Cat in the ancient fairy-tale retold by Madame d'Aulnoy. The White Cat was in fact a bewitched princess. She enabled a neighbouring King's son to be successful in various trials imposed by the King on his three sons to help him to decide on the selection of his heir. When the successful prince asked the White Cat what he could do for her, she said that nothing would satisfy her but that he should behead her with his own hands. Although naturally somewhat reluctant, he did so, when she and all her court regained their human shapes. In some versions they all carried catskin cloaks.

The idea of the human being in animal form has always fascinated the romancers and even today in the midst of all the books about real cats one meets stories like Paul Gallico's *Jennie,* about the little boy who became a cat, proving that mankind is still dreaming of how nice it would be to possess magical powers. Very different from Jennie is Tobermory in the story of that name by 'Saki'. Tobermory acquired the gift of human speech and with a cynical (if one can without offence apply the word to cats) disregard of the consequences, used his gift with devastating effect on members of a house-party. He was, as Saki describes him, a 'beyond' cat.

In a different mode from Saki's gentle, if biting, wit, is the sparkling humour of Sandy Wilson in *This is Sylvia,* one of the most entertaining 'human-cat' stories ever written. Sandy Wilson's heroine is in the direct succession from Minette, the socialite heroine of Balzac's *Peines de coeur d'une chatte Anglaise* who also appears in a more charming sequel by P.-J. Stahl. Grandville's illustrations to the two latter (illust 57 and 58 and pages 112 and 114) must surely have inspired Sandy Wilson's own brilliantly witty illustrations to *Sylvia* (pages 115 and 116).

All these magical or mystical cats or cat-humans of the imagination have something more or less whimsical about them and are thus remote from the divine cats of Egypt, who, as a vital element in the religion of the country, had nothing humorous in their nature or in their cult. Perhaps modern man is slightly ashamed of being a cat-worshipper and has to wrap his devotion up in a cloak of laughter to disguise it. Yet the modern mystical cat can certainly look up to the cats of ancient Egypt as his or her spiritual ancestors. As everyone knows, cats occupied a position of unique importance in Egypt – witness the numerous images of Bast or Pasht, the cat-goddess with her attendant cats, together with innumerable bronzes of cats, cat amulets and the like. Herodotus' account of cats in Egypt and of the annual festival at the city of Bubastis, the centre of cat worship and the principal burial place of the cats, is well supported by Diodorus Siculus, the Greek historian who was born in Sicily and travelled in Egypt about the middle of the first century B.C., by Cicero and, indeed, by modern Egyptologists, which is more than can be said of a great many of his tall stories.

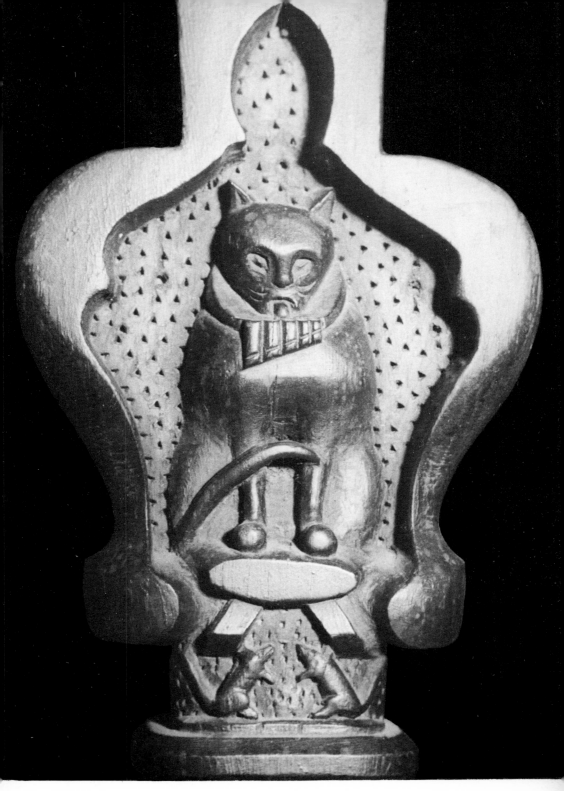

1. Cat plays panpipes to lure mice; poppyhead, Farthingstone Church, Northamptonshire (p. 37)

2. Cat lifting a mouse out of a trap;
bench-end, North Cadbury Church,
Somerset (p. 40)

3. Cat with mouse; bench-end,
Upper Sheringham Church, Norfolk

4. Cat with a mouse in her mouth; misericord, Winchester Cathedral

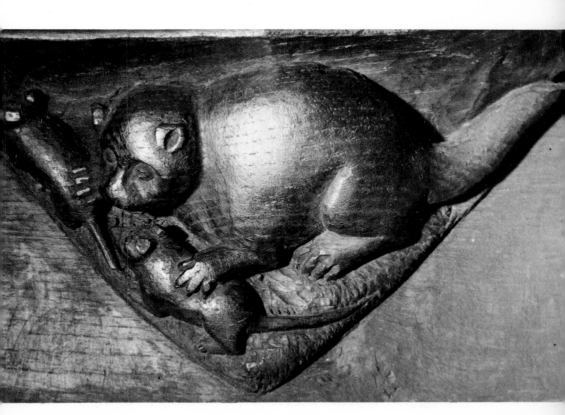

5. Cat with two mice; misericord, Beverley Minster (p. 40)

6. Two cats sparring; corner of cornice of Evercreech Church, Somerset (p. 40)

7. Cat with a mouse in his mouth; capital of pillar in the Chapterhouse, Lichfield Cathedral

People have been sometimes puzzled by Shakespeare's two epithets for the cat – 'harmless' and 'necessary'. In Egypt the cat was necessary on the highest plane of existence, namely religion, but Shylock was doubtless referring to its mousing capacity. This was universally recognized. The Welsh Prince, Hywel Dda, established the place of cats in his Codes of laws; he made it quite clear, for instance, that the cat who kept the King's barn clear of mice was an extremely important functionary. In the *Ancren Riwle* or *Ancrene Wisse*, the unknown author of a devotional code for anchoresses, among them a sisterhood in Ireland, recognizes the need for a cat as companion: 'Ye mine leove sustren ne schulen haben no Best bute Kat one.'

This idea, expressed in the thirteenth century, finds an echo in the words of Mark Twain towards the end of the nineteenth:

A home without a cat, and a well-fed, well-petted and properly revered cat, may be a perfect home, *perhaps*, but how can it prove its title?

One would have liked to include among necessary cats, a 'Who's Who' of official cats. Alas, the list could never be complete and an incomplete one would be invidious. Most offices, barracks, storehouses and post offices have cats on their staffs. Very properly, H.M. Postmaster General has an arrangement for cats employed in his Department to have ration allowances.

The Home Office have a Manx cat, Peta, who was presented to them in 1964 by the Lieutenant-Governor of the Isle of Man. There has been a succession of Home Office cats, mostly male and all named Peter, since 1883. (So far as can be ascertained, no Home Secretary has been called Peter.) Peta has, of course, a ration allowance. Official cats are also employed by the London Museum and the Wallace Collection.

The National Printing Office of France keeps a staff of cats to protect their papers from rats and mice. Her Majesty's Stationery Office does not. In giving this information in 1965, Mr Niall MacDermot, Financial Secretary to the Treasury, expressed the hope that this did not imply that British Government publications were more indigestible than French ones.

One famous official, or perhaps semi-official, cat was Mike, who helped to keep the gate at the British Museum from February 1909 to January 1929, a period of nearly twenty years. Mike was apostrophized by several distinguished Museum colleagues and, together with his sponsor, Black Jack, of the Reading Room, has been accorded a short section later on in this volume.

It has sometimes been said that certain human ailments such as asthma have been caused, or aggravated, by the presence of cats. Be that as it may, it has to be set against the cat's value as a destroyer of disease carriers such as rats. Indian villages where there are a lot of cats are said to be freer of cholera than villages without cats; and when the Japanese were starting a campaign to abolish bubonic plague, one of their first actions was to import a cargo of cats.

So much for 'necessary'; but what of 'harmless'? Few people can forgive cats for their ferocious treatment of birds. And does the mistress of the house regard as harmless those unrestrained claw-sharpening attacks on the best brocade chair covers? Further, 'harmless' is scarcely the word to describe the cat who, albeit with the best motives in the world, lies on a baby in its cot and nearly smothers it. Perhaps Shylock had not thought of birds, brocade and babies and was merely comparing the slight harm done to humans by cats in general with the appalling injury he was about to do Antonio.

It is of course true that we more often hear of harm done *to* than *by* cats. The sinister fate of Mr Brooks's cats as related by Sam Weller to Mr Pickwick is a case in point and reminds one of the story of the pie-shop's dismissed waiter who returned to the shop late one Saturday evening when it was crowded with hungry customers and flung on to the counter half a dozen dead cats, with the sinister remark: 'That's the lot, Guvnor.' One prefers the tale of the cat who ate a piece of cheese and then went and sat in front of a mouse-hole with 'baited' breath.

It is not uncommon for a famous author to have brought fame to an individual who scarcely deserved it, nor for an artist to have immortalized the features of a mediocrity. Does a man's own fame descend – or should one say ascend? – to his cat? Did Sir Winston Churchill's cat become famous because of his illustrious master, or because of being drawn in various attractive attitudes by Sir William Nicholson? The Graham family's cat must have been anything but a nonentity, if Hogarth's portrait is to be believed. But rarely has a truly famous cat – famous, that is, in his own right – been painted. Who, for instance, has painted or drawn Mourka, the hero-cat of Stalingrad, immortalized in a leader in *The Times*?

The writers and artists whose work appears in these pages speak – or exhibit – for themselves and no attempt has been made here or in the chapters on the cat in art and religion, on inn-signs or in the nursery, to make a critical evaluation of that work. The really remarkable thing about it is its variety – the innumerable facets and qualities of the cat as subject and model which have been displayed.

Those who have lost much-loved cats – and who has not? – can be astonished at the pain and grief which such a loss brings with it. Michael Joseph, in his book *Cat's Company*, rates companionship of man as a cat's greatest need. To man, there is no companionship quite like it. 'Sometimes,' wrote Théophile Gautier of a cat, 'he will sit upon the carpet in front of you looking at you with eyes so melting, so caressing and so human, that they almost frighten you, for it is impossible to believe that a soul is not there.' In an epitaph written in Latin by Dr Jortin, Archdeacon of London in the eighteenth century, and imitated in English by

Graham Tomson, a cat on her arrival in the Nether Regions petitions
Proserpine to let her go home for one night a year:

> Once more to see my home and mistress dear,
> And purr these grateful accents in her ear:
> 'Thy faithful cat, thy poor departed slave,
> Still loves her mistress, e'en beyond the grave.'

Perhaps, after all, 'harmless' and 'necessary' are the most just epithets to
apply to a cat.

'The cat did it', by George Cruikshank

A cat's a cat for a' that

CAT. A well-known carnivorous quadruped which has long been domesticated, being kept to destroy mice and as a house pet. The name is common European of unknown origin. In England there have been variations of spelling such as CATTE, KATTE, KAT or CAT.

CATTA appears in Martial before A.D. 100, but Ciceronian Latin has FELES.

Κάττα is found in Byzantine Greek and later καττος, but classical Greek has αἴλουρος.

The word, or sound, 'cat' signifies the animal throughout Europe and comes from the Romanic forms CATTUS and CATTA. Hence CHAT (French); GATTO (It.); GATO (Sp.); Γάττος (mod. Gr.); KATER (m), KATZE (f) (Ger.); KATTUZ (m), KATTÔN (f) (Old Teutonic); KOT (Russ., etc.); KOTKA (old Slav., etc.); KATTI (Finnish); CAT (Gaelic).

The O.E.D. points out that these forms show extensive communication of the word but do not fix the original source. The quotation from Martial contains what appears to be the earliest use, *circa* A.D. 75 while the poet was in Rome, viz.

> *Pannonicas nobis numquam dedit Umbria cattas:*
> *Mavult haec domino mittere dona Pudens.*

Aulus Pudens was a friend of Martial's and served as a Centurion in Pannonia. He was a native of Umbria, and the epigram means that he preferred to send to his patron in Rome other gifts than Pannonian cats. These gifts are mentioned in a previous epigram and were golden orioles and green woodpeckers. Capps, Page and Rouse, in their edition of the Epigrams, declare that no one knows what 'cattae' were.

The O.E.D. observes that the earliest home of the domestic cat was Egypt and that 'the name is generally sought in the same quarter'. The French writer Champfleury (the pen-name of Jules Fleury-Husson), who published a book on cats in 1868, said that the ancient Egyptian name for 'cat' was 'Chaou'. However, Professor Heinrich Brugsch, the eminent German Egyptologist, writing in 1889, pointed out that in inscriptions on newly excavated pyramids of the fifth and sixth Dynasties, the cat appears under the designation MIU (or, if female, MIU-T); in the last centuries before our era, this had become EMU – all of which are delightfully onomatopoeic.

Professor Brugsch mentions the word 'Chatul' as the word for cat in

Judeo-Aramaic ('Chatûl' in the Talmud) but observes that the domestic cat is nowhere mentioned in the Bible. Still searching for the origin of the word 'cat', Brugsch notes that in the Nubian language used in ancient Ethiopia, the normal word for the domestic cat was KADIS. An even more famous German Egyptologist, Professor Karl Richard Lepsius, referring to this word in his Nubian Grammar, declares that from it derive the Arabic QITT, the Turkish KADI, and thence 'Catus', 'Gatto', 'Chat', and 'Katze'; and from this he reaches the conclusion that Ethiopia was the cat's country of origin from which it spread to the rest of the world. While not firmly endorsing this view, Brugsch suggests that there is support for it in the habit of the ancient Ethiopians, of naming their princes after various animals, in particular SCHABA-KŌ, which means 'Cat', 'Lord'; and he quotes as an analogy the names of certain Egyptian kings, – PMI, or PMIU, i.e. 'Cat'. Evidence that the first cats to reach China (about A.D. 300) came from Egypt is provided by the fact that these cats were given the name 'Mao' or 'Miu'. ('Mao', cat, must not be confused with the name of the ruler of Communist China. The former is pronounced with a level tone, the latter with a rising tone.)

In mediaeval Latin, the cat was sometimes referred to as 'Murilegus', 'Muriceps', or 'Musio', because of its anti-mouse propensities; and Bossewell (q.v.) anglicizes the word into 'Musion'.

The Greeks do not appear to have been interested in or to have heard of 'Cat the Mousekiller', nor does Herodotus, who studied and wrote on the Egyptian cult of cats, seem to have noticed the onomatopoeic name – however, with their Hellenic perception of beauty they found the perfect name in αἴλουρος, the animal which has a tail with a wavy motion.

An alternative Greek word for cat is γαλη, but this can mean either weasel or cat. Liddell and Scott translate γαλη as 'marten-cat or pole-cat'.

In the *Ecclesiazusae,* Aristophanes, writing in 393 B.C., tells us that ἡ διαξειεν γαλη – i.e. if a cat crosses your path, it's a sign of bad luck; and in 319 B.C. Theophrastus (in *Characters* No. XVI Sec. 2) using the same word, gives a slightly different rendering of the saying, viz: την ὁδον ἐαν ὑπερδραμη γαλη, μη προτερον, which might be rendered

> If any cat across your purposed path should run,
> you'll get no further on the journey you've begun.

In either of these cases γαλη could be used to mean weasel or pole-cat; but when Theocritus fifty years later wrote in 270 B.C., in his 15th Idyll, *Gorgo and Praxinoë* – αἱ γαλεαι μαλακως χρηζοντι καθευδειν – all cats like a cushioned couch – he surely can only mean the domestic cat, which may by his time have become common in Sicily, where he lived and wrote.

There is, however, something of a mystery about the cat in Hellas, so little is to be found about it in classical Greek literature. That the animal was known is clear from the base of a pillar with sculptured relief showing two young men inciting a cat and dog to fight, which archaeologists attribute to the end of the sixth century B.C. According to Graham Tomson, there is an Athenian vase of the best period showing the cat as a mouser and there is a fresco in the Candia Museum, Crete, showing a cat hunting a pheasant, attributed to 1500 B.C.

But there is no ancient Greek origin for the modern Greek proverb – Λειπ᾽ ὁ γάτος, καὶ χορευουν τα ποντικια – 'When the cat's gone off, the mice go dancing'. This proverb is to be found in most languages; one of its pleasantest forms in English may be found in the Harleian MS 3362 of A.D. 1470 where it is rendered 'The Mows Lordchypyth where a cat ys nawt'.

What sort of a mouse it is which accepts the cat's invitation when 'the cat invites the mouse to a feast', as Thomas Fuller writes in *Gnomologia* in 1732, it is hard to say, but it is scarcely the mouse of the proverb 'A bashful cat makes a proud mouse'.

There is quite a bunch of proverbs and sayings on the cat–mouse connection. To Cheshire is attributed 'Did you ever know a kitling bring a mouse to the old cat?', signifying children are not always ready to support their parents – a sardonic view of life to which Alice's attention would surely have been drawn by the Cheshire Cat had he known the saying.

'The borrowed cat catches no mice', which is said to come from Japan, means that no one is going to lend his best mouser – or his best tools. And if you want a cat to catch mice you mustn't hide its claws – proverbially – 'A gloved catte can catch no myse', which is to be found in *Houres of Recreation* by James Sandford published in 1572.

Arabia produces the pleasant – 'The cat that is always crying catches nothing', a remark which may have inspired the idea of belling the cat.

The French say '*à bon chat. bon rat*'; according to John Heywood, writing in 1546, the English version is 'cat after kynde good mouse hunt'.

That cats know on which side their bread is buttered is enshrined in *Fecunda Ratis* by Egbert von Lüttich, writing in 1023, where he states '*Ad cuius veniat scit cattus lingere barbam*'.

In 1300 this was pleasantly rendered in English in the *Proverbs* of Hending (ed. Schleich) in MS Anglia 51 270 – 'Well wote badde [i.e. cat] wose berde he lickith'.

'To walk like a cat on hot bricks' is given in Ray's proverbs in 1678 in the form, 'To go like a cat upon a hot bake-stone'; suggesting that there was food at the end of the journey. To like something 'as a cat likes mustard' is also quoted by Ray but does not seem to have survived to modern times.

Cotgrave tells us, in 1611, 'the cat is hungry when a crust contents her' – a sternness which few ailurophiles of today would practise – while

David Fergusson in 1595 cites the Scottish proverb – 'Catis eatis quhilk hissies spairs'.

In *Remains* in 1605 William Camden writes 'an old cat laps as much milk as a young', but the stern Cotgrave prefers 'the lickorous [i.e. lecherous] cat hath many a rap'. A kindlier view is taken by Thomas Fuller (again in *Gnomologia*) who wrote 'when the maid leaves open the door, blame not the cat'.

The cat appears in numerous saws without the question of 'cattiness' being involved – 'when all candels be out, all cats be grey', says John Heywood in his *Proverbs* in 1546.

Sometime before 1384 John Wyclif wrote 'many men of lawe bi there suteltes turnen the cat in the panne' – here, of course, he means that these sly gentry make things appear the opposite of reality.

Much later, in the early eighteenth century, the Vicar of Bray said:

> When George in pudding-time came o'er
> And moderate men looked big, Sir,
> I turned a cat-in-pan once more
> And so became a Whig, Sir.

Various explanations of this expression are given by Nares in his *Glossary of English Phrases*. One writer in the *Gentleman's Magazine* in 1754, conjectures that 'cat' was originally 'cate', or 'cake', a derivation which is not favoured by the *O.E.D.* Another, with remarkable ingenuity, traces it to *Catipani*, whom he supposes to be a perfidious tribe in Calabria and Apulia. But *Catipanus*, or *Capitaneus*, was the title of an official who held office under the Byzantine Emperors. One Hoffman gives a list of these *Catipani*. Du Cange suggests that the phrase came from the Byzantine Greek – κατεπανω – or possibly from καταπαντοκρατορα, meaning 'second to the Chief Commander' – Chief of Staff, in fact – though how this could come to signify either the trickster, with Wyclif, or the turncoat, with the Vicar of Bray, is hard to follow. Even the *O.E.D.* has to admit that the true origin of the phrase is unknown. A variant found in *Follie's Anatomie*, by H. Hutton, in 1619, namely, 'turne the cat i' th' band', does not suggest any more plausible origin. The *English Dialect Dictionary* gives 'Turning head over heels over a bar while holding on to it'. Despite the *O.E.D.*, to 'turn cate *in panem*', i.e. to turn a dainty into a piece of plain bread, has its attractions.

'A cat may look at a king' is another saying without an unassailably authenticated origin. J. Heywood quotes it in 1562, in the form, 'a cat maie look on a king, ye know'. Bailey describes it as 'a saucy proverb, generally made use of by pragmatical persons'. The saying has a German form, '*Darf doch die Katze der Kaiser anzehen*', which is said to have originated with a remark of the Emperor Maximilian I in 1517, when he visited the shop of one Hieronymus Resch, who made wood-cuts and whose cat lay at ease on the table, staring suspiciously at the Emperor throughout the interview.

The view expressed by Aristophanes and Theophrastus in the fourth century B.C., that you were in for some ill-luck if a cat crossed your path, seems to be contradicted today, at least so far as black cats are concerned. T. F. Thistleton-Dyer, for instance, in *English Folklore*, quotes the couplet:

> Whenever the cat of the house is black,
> The lasses of lovers will have no lack.

This could be connected with the belief that witches' cats were usually black and that from witches one obtained love-potions. It could hardly have anything to do with that other ancient warning – 'When weasel and cat make marriage, evil presage'.

The cat has been responsible for more adages than almost any other animal, and it would be tedious to repeat them all, but here are a few of the more interesting:

To be a cat's-paw To be someone's tool. This comes from the fable in which a monkey seizes hold of a cat and snatches the roasted chestnuts from the fire with the cat's-paw (illust 44). '*Tire-moi ces marrons,*' says the monkey to the cat in La Fontaine. Some have thought that 'cat' here is short for '*catellus*', a whelp or puppy, since in older forms of the story the victim was a dog. In an Arabian version of the same tale, it is a roast crab which the monkey makes the cat pull from the bars, not chestnuts.

To live under the sign of the cat's foot To be henpecked.

To shoot the cat To be sick, after drink taken.

To whip the cat A game in which a simpleton on one side of a pond has a rope tied round his waist, while the other end of the rope is taken across the pond and tied to the tail of a cat. The cat is then whipped to make it run and pull the man into the pond. To the simpleton's astonishment the cat succeeds in dragging him through the pond, the power having, of course, been supplied by several husky fellows on the rope.

The cat has a gale of wind in her tail This refers to the nautical belief that if a cat on board ship is more playful than usual and rushes about, there is a storm coming up.

To nurse the cat To be idle.

Cat in barrel A barbarous amusement said to have been indulged in by the people of Kelso, in Roxburghshire, in which a cat is put in a barrel partly filled with soot. This is slung up between two high poles and belaboured until the barrel is smashed up and the cat, demented, escapes from between the broken staves, only to be finished off cruelly by the crowd. This 'amusement' is described in *Kelso*, by Lazarus, in 1789 and by Brand in *Popular Antiquities*.

Cat-o'-nine-tails   A lash. Also an earwig (which is sometimes called a Cat-o'-two-tails).

Cat washing dishes   Sunlight reflected on the ceiling or walls from a pail of water.

To let the cat out of the bag   If someone is so foolish as to buy a pig in a poke, a bystander who gives the show away – i.e. discloses that the bag contains not a sucking-pig but a cat – is said to let the cat out of the bag. Hence to blurt out secrets.

There are a number of sayings referring to the cat winking. 'Let the catte winke and leat the mouse ronne' is found in Heywood in 1546. Both Ray in 1678 and Fuller in 1732, have it as 'When the cat winketh, little wots the mouse what the cat thinketh'; and in 1609, Rowlands, in *A Whole Crew of Kind Gossips*, has 'The cat ofte winkes, and yet she is not blinde'.

'Care killed the cat' means merely that care is a killer and will even finish off a creature which has nine lives – a cat being reputed to be singularly tenacious of life. 'Nine', of course, is one of the mystical numbers, a 'trinity of trinities'; for this reason, a cat-o'-nine-tails is supposed to be especially sacred and effective. One of the earliest references to a cat's nine lives is by Shakespeare; in *Romeo and Juliet*, Tybalt (the name given to the cat in the mediaeval romance of *Reynard the Fox*) asks, 'What would'st thou have with me?' and Mercutio answers, 'Good King of Cats, nothing but one of your nine lives'.

Some of the phrases which have become commonplace are corruptions. Such a one is 'Cat's-cradle', which is a corruption of 'cratch-cradle', 'cratch' being an anglicized version of '*crèche*', a manger or crib. A cratch-cradle is, of course, the manger of the Infant Jesus.

'Cat and Fiddle' is another phrase developed by corruption, but it is a term with such wide ramifications as to need a chapter to itself.

The 'Cat-water' or 'Catte-water', at Plymouth, is a singular distortion of the original, based on a mis-interpretation of French. At one time the castle at the mouth of the Plym was known as the '*Château*'. It was thought advisable, during the French wars, to anglicize it and some wiseacre decided that it came from '*chat*' and '*eau*' – hence, 'Cat-water'!

A motto such as 'Touch not the Cat but a glove' is not, properly speaking, derived from corruption. According to Brewer, the words are the motto of Clan Mackintosh, whose crest is a wild-cat, or 'cat-a-mountain salient guardant proper' with, as supporters, two cats proper. The whole, says Brewer, is a pun on the word 'Catti', the Teutonic settlers of Caithness. The word 'but' is used in the sense of 'without' and the word 'glove' is probably 'glaive', i.e. broadsword and the whole means that it is not safe to strike the Clan Chattan unless you have a sword in your hand.

The cat has been used occasionally in political lampoons, the most famous of which cost its author, Collingbourne, his life. Holinshed wrote of this incident that Richard III executed 'a poore gentleman called Callingbourne, for making a small rime of three of his . . . councellors, . . . lord Louell, sir Richard Ratcliffe . . . and sir William Catesbie. . . .

> The Cat, the Rat, and Louell our dog,
> Rule all England under an hog.

Meaning by the hog, the . . . wild boare, which was the King's cognisance.'

The cat has been called by many names in its time. 'Puss' or 'pussy', which is the commonest, is of unknown origin; it belongs more properly to the hare. The most attractive and indeed probable derivation is Pasht or Bast. 'Grimalkin', used often in describing a witch's cat or familiar, is a combination of 'grey' and 'Malkin', the latter being an obsolete diminutive for Matilda or Maud and itself sometimes used of a cat. The origin of the homely Scottish 'Baudrons' is not known but may have a connection with the word 'badde' used for a cat in the *Proverbs* of Hending. Its earliest appearance is about 1450 and it comes pleasantly in Burns' poem 'Willie's Wife'.

While the name 'Tom' for a male cat seems to have originated about the year 1450 from no one knows where, 'Tabby', occasionally used for a female, is the term once used for a striped or watered silk taffeta and thus applied to any cat with a stripy coat. The word 'tabby' itself comes originally from *attābiy*, the name of a quarter in Baghdad, where a certain type of silk was made. Its modern application to the female only is probably due to a confusion with the name Tabitha.

There are too many secondary meanings of 'cat' and too many cat-compounds, to list more than a very few. A trivet, for instance, is sometimes called a cat, because it always stands firmly on its (three) legs – strange, when a cat always lands securely on all four. 'Cat' also figures in a number of games; it is the piece of wood used in the game of 'tip-cat' and frequently it means the game itself. Sometimes it is a cake of clay, salt and meal used to lure pigeons, particularly strangers, into a dove-cot. It can be a ball of clay mixed with coal for burning; or a mixture of clay and straw for putting between laths when building a mud-wall; it may be a handful of straw; or even a small piece of rag to put between the handle of a pot and the hook on which it hangs to raise the pot further from the fire. It is the name often used for a quart pewter pot, a brown vegetable dye, a spiteful woman, a device for laming cavalry horses, a wanton, a movable pent-house used in old-time sieges, a lofty work in fortifications (sometimes known as a 'cavalier'), a small coal-carrying coaster. There used to be a riddle current among North Sea pilots and their friends: 'When did the mouse catch the cat?' Answer: 'When the cat (collier) ran aground on the Mouse' (a sandbank in the estuary of the Thames). It is said that Sir Richard Whittington made his fortune bringing coals from Newcastle to London in cats – hence the story of Dick and his 'cat'.

More entertaining, perhaps, than these meanings of the word, are 'cat-compounds' – where parts of a cat's body mean anything but what they seem. From top to tail, some of these are:

Cat-head	a beam projecting on both bows of a ship for raising the anchor. An ironstone nodule. A square wooden box for collecting wind.
Cat's-head	a kind of apple. The knuckle-end of a leg of mutton.
Cat's-hair	the down on the faces of beardless boys.
Cat-locks	*Eriophorum vaginatum* (Cotton Grass).
Cat-scalp	clay ironstone.
Cat's-brains	clayey soil containing small stones.
Cat's-ear	*Hieracium pilosella* (Mouse-ear).
Cat-face	a mark on lumber-wood; the front of the top of a cabriole leg at the centre of the frame of a seat.
Cat's-face	*Viola tricolor* (Heartsease).
Cat's-eye	a gem; today also a reflector in the road.
Cat Chop	*Mesembryanthemum felinum* (*Faucaria felina*).
Cats-tongues	a meagre dish or meal.
Cat's-leg	nonsense.
Cat's-foot	*Nepeta glechoma* (Ground Ivy).
Cat's-feet	marks left on linen after it has been washed and dried.
Cat's-paw	a faint breeze just ruffling the surface of the sea. (See also 'To be a cat's paw', p. 24.)
Cat's-claws	Cat's-clover = *Lotus corniculatus* (Bird's-foot Trefoil).
Cat-back	a rope for hauling the cat-hook in securing the anchor.
Cat-kidney	a game something like cricket or tip-cat.
Cat's-tail (or *Cat's-spear*)	*Typha latifolia* (Reed-mace); also *Equisetum* (Horse-tail).

Among the more amusing 'cat' birds are:

Catbrandtail	the Redstart.
Cat-bill	the Woodpecker.
Cat-gull	the Herring Gull.
Cat-swallow	the Black Tern.
Cat-ogle	the Eagle-Owl.
Sea-mew	the Common Gull – so called because of its cry (*cf.* German Möwe.)

And what of caterpillar? Has this anything to do with cats? In fact, caterpillars seem to have suggested both cats and dogs in turn. Ernest Weekley tells us that the word is corrupted by folk-etymology from Old French, *chatepeleuse*, 'a corne-devouring mite or weevell' (as interpreted by Cotgrave). But the word, says Weekley, probably means 'woolly cat'. Today, the French word for caterpillar is *chenille*, a derivative of *chien*. So one can take one's choice.

Anyone who has persevered in reading so far may well complain that it is 'raining cats and dogs'. Brewer says this is a corruption of 'catedupe', a waterfall. Someone else has suggested κατα δοξας or, 'contrary to experience'. An egregious commentator, named John Bellenden Ker (of whom more elsewhere), early in the nineteenth century derived it from a species of crazy Dutch which later critics say he invented himself. On the whole, Brewer has it on points.

C was a lovely Pussy Cat; its eyes were large & pale;
And on its back it had some stripes,
and several on his tail.

The cat in art, secular and sacred

While the cat as model has inspired the carver, the sculptor and the potter to a greater extent than the painter or draughtsman, some of the earliest examples of the cat in art are to be found in drawings and paintings. As might be expected, Egypt provides many ancient drawings of cats, one of the most delightful being the artist's trial piece done on flaked limestone, reproduced in illust 9. Flaked limestone was used as today one would use a sketch book. The drawing is in terracotta-coloured paint and the date is late New Kingdom (1580 to 1100 B.C.). The sketch was doubtless made in preparation for a wall-painting and has such life and dash about it that it is hard to believe in its antiquity.

While the artist has given the drawing all the natural dignity which is every cat's due, there is a quality of affection in it which convinces one that it is a portrait of a well-loved friend.

Cats, both as domestic pets and hunters, appear on a number of Egyptian wall-paintings. There is a painting in the tomb of a sculptor named Apy at Thebes, in which an obviously loved cat with a silver ring in her ear sits under the chair of her mistress, Dowesmiset, while a kitten sits on the knee of her husband Apy pulling at his sleeve (c. 1400 B.C.). In another painting at Thebes, a cat looks up while gnawing a bone under the chair of Mutemuia, who is sitting watching her husband, Kenro, playing a game which looks like a mixture of chess, backgammon and halma (reign of Rameses II, XIXth Dynasty, 1292–1225 B.C.).

Egyptian pet cats apparently enjoyed sitting under their mistresses' chairs, for in another tomb at Thebes, in a painting of a feast, a little ginger cat is shown under a lady's chair. The cat has been described as 'one of the prettiest and most delicately executed of the many presentations of the subject in Theban tombs'. The cat has a pink tongue and a very long tail (c. 1400 B.C.). In yet another tomb, of the reign of Tuthmosis III, of the XVIIth Dynasty, in the middle of the fifteenth century B.C., the pet cat of Tui, the wife of a harbourmaster named May, is shown under her chair. Here the cat suffers the indignity of a leash by which she is tied to the leg of the chair, so that she is forced to pull against it to get at a bowl of food, while endeavouring with one paw to detach the cord from the chair-leg.

The ancient Egyptians appear to have been the only people who used cats' skill as hunters to aid them in the chase. One of the most famous wall-paintings of about 1400 B.C. (in the British Museum) depicts Nebamen standing on a papyrus skiff hunting waterfowl with a boomerang-stick.

His wife Hatshepsut stands behind him and his daughter squats in the skiff, holding on to his leg, while his cat pounces on and retrieves the birds as her master brings them down (illust 8).

This theme was, however, also adopted by Cretan and Mycenean artists. There is in the museum at Candia a fresco (illust 16) of the late Minoan period (about 1500 B.C.) from Hagia Triada, showing a cat stalking a pheasant. (In their wall-paintings the Egyptians did not use the true fresco technique in which the painting becomes part of the substance of the wall. This was a prominent feature of the prehistoric Minoan culture earlier than 1500 B.C.) Two of the finest Mycenean weapon blades bear similar designs in flat inlay – a type to be found on daggers from the tomb of Queen Aah Hotep of Egypt, the date being about 1600 B.C., contemporary with Mycenae. The designs on these blades depict cats hunting ducks in thickets of papyrus, beside a stream in which fish can be seen swimming.

After the early Egyptian paintings, a long period seems to have elapsed before artists again put cats on paper or canvas. Both Leonardo da Vinci and Dürer in the late fifteenth or early sixteenth centuries have given us striking cat drawings, although these are in a sense incidental to the main subject (illust 20 and 19). The same applies to Rembrandt's cat in an engraving of the Virgin and Child executed in 1654 (illust 21).

A cat appears prominently in Albrecht Dürer's famous engraving of 1504 which depicts the Fall of Man (illust 19). In his *Life and Art of Albrecht Dürer*, Professor Erwin Panofsky tells us that Dürer's contemporaries would have appreciated the parallelism of the 'tense relation between Adam and Eve' and the tenseness of the cat crouching to spring on the mouse. He suggests that such a feature would not immediately strike a modern observer. This is highly probable, particularly as the cat does not appear poised for a spring, but has the aspect of complete contentment and neighbourliness proper to the Garden of Eden.

In the Middle Ages there was a theory, first advanced in the twelfth century, which attributed men's characteristics to the four 'humours' or 'temperaments'. These were supposed to be fluids which pervaded the body and a man was 'sanguine', 'choleric', 'phlegmatic', or 'melancholic' according to which of these mysterious fluids was in the ascendant in him. A doctrine widely accepted by scholars connected the Fall of Man with this theory and postulated that in the perfect human being the four humours were perfectly balanced. With the Fall the balance was lost and every man's personality was thereafter determined by a prevailing humour; the character of the various animals however was governed by these humours from the beginning. Panofsky points out that in Dürer's engraving the four humours are symbolized by animals, the rabbit representing the sanguine, the elk the melancholic, the ox the phlegmatic and the cat the choleric and that these would have been easily recognized by educated men in the sixteenth century. While this may be true, it is hard to attribute a choleric temperament to the charming cat of the engraving.

The cat also appears in the 'topsy-turvy' world popular in the Middle Ages and illustrated by such artists as Peter Brueghel the Elder in his painting of Netherlandish proverbs in 1559. The cat is depicted as being 'belled' – *Desen hangt de cat de bel aen* (illust 22).

Cat portraits did not become common until the nineteenth century, but some do exist at a much earlier date, although there is often little to authenticate a likeness. There is in the Guildhall the engraving of a painting by one Reginald Elstrack of Sir Richard (Dick) Whittington and his cat. Elstrack's painting was dated about 1590 and it is therefore highly improbable, as Whittington lived from 1358 to 1423, that the cat is a genuine portrait of the original. In the picture, the Lord Mayor is shown with his right hand resting on a cat's head. It is related that the hand originally rested on a skull, but that the plate was cut and a cat substituted in deference to the public's belief in the story that it was a cat which led Dick on his first steps to making his fortune.

In Welbeck Abbey, there is a portrait of Henry Wriothesley, third Earl of Southampton, with his black and white cat on the window-sill behind him. The picture was painted in 1602 or 1603 when the Earl was imprisoned in the Tower. Thomas Pennant, who was an antiquarian as well as naturalist and traveller, writing towards the end of the eighteenth century, related that while Wriothesley was in the Tower, 'he was surprised by a visit from his favourite cat, which had forced its way to the Tower, and, as tradition says, reached his master by descending the chimney of his apartment'.

Even more famous is the portrait of Sir Henry Wyat and his cat, painted in 1532 after the style of Holbein. Sir Henry (father of the more famous Sir Thomas) was imprisoned as a Lancastrian supporter by Richard III and released later by Henry VII. According to an old manuscript among the Wyat papers in the possession of the Earl of Romney, written by Thomas Scott of Egreston –

. . . . hee was imprisoned often, once in a cold and narrow Tower, where hee had neither bed to lie on, nor cloaths sufficient to warme him, nor meate for his mouth; hee had starved there, had not God (who sent a crowe to feede his Prophet) sent this, His, and his country's martyr, a cat both to feede and warme him: – itt was his own relation unto them from whom I had it; a cat one day came down into the Dungeon unto him; and as it were offered herself unto him, hee was glad of her, laid her in his bosome to warme him, and by making much of her, won her love; after this, shee would come every day unto him, divers times, and when shee could gett one, bring him a pigeon; hee complain'd to his keeper of his cold, and short fare, the answer was hee durst not better itt; but said Sir Henry, if I can provide any, will you promise to dresse itt for mee; I may well enough (said the keeper) you are safe for that matter – and being urged againe, promised him, and kept his promise – dressed for him from time to time such pigeons as his Accator the cat provided for him. Sir Henry Wyat in his prosperity, for this, would ever make much of a cat, as other men will of their spaniels, or hounds; and perhaps you shall not find his picture anywhere but (like Sir Christopher Hatton with his dog) with a cat beside him; . . . .

Another portrait in which a cat is an important feature is a picture of the famous Andrea Doria, Genoese admiral, painted shortly before his death in 1560 and until recently attributed to Titian. The aged admiral sits in his chair with a well-liking, solid cat sitting on the table beside him, and it is said that his favourite cat used to accompany him on all his voyages.

J. Theodore Bent, however, in his *Genoa: How the Republic Rose and Fell*, records this curious tale:

Of the old prince's resentful passion a quaint story is told, probably not true, but proving by its existence the spirit which men attributed to him. It is affirmed that for the remainder of his days the prince always kept a cat near him, to remind him of the fallen Fieschi's badge, and that when a fit of rage came on him he would mercilessly beat this cat with his stick, by way of symbolizing the punishment he would visit on his foes. There is an old picture in his palace of Fazzuolo, still hanging in his own private room, representing old Andrea in his ninety-third year. A meagre, worn-out old man he is, with scarce a gleam of fire in his sunken eye; by his side sits a well-favoured cat. Whether this was the unfortunate animal or not which acted the part of scape-goat, report says not.

There are two cat portraits which stand pre-eminent and which may be regarded as authentic likenesses. One is the famous cat in the picture of the Graham children, painted by Hogarth in 1742, now in the Tate Gallery (illust 26). Of this cat Sir Kenneth Clark remarks:

Hogarth enjoyed painting this cat so much that the Graham children look hollow and lifeless beside her. She is the embodiment of cockney vitality, alert, and adventurous – a sort of Nell Gwynn among cats.

The other is the Grand Duke of Moscovy's cat, engraved in 1663 by the famous etcher, Wenceslaus Hollar of Bohemia, who worked chiefly in London. The exquisite workmanship in this engraving compels one's belief in its being a true likeness. To make doubly sure, however, the artist has entitled it *Le vray portrait du chat du grand Duc de Moscouie* (illust 24).

The artists who produced these cat portraits were not, properly speaking, 'cat' painters. The pictures were incidents in their paintings and drawings; the subjects happened to include cats. There have been, however, one or two artists whose whole artistic output was devoted to cats. The two best known are the English Louis Wain and the Hungarian Gottfried Mind. Mind, the earlier of the two, was born in 1768 and actually lived in Berne. With the exception of bears, which he occasionally drew, Mind appears to have thought cats the only subject worthy of his notice. His gift won him

8. Wall painting from
tomb at Thebes,
Egypt; Nebamen the
fowler with his cat
(*circa* 1400 BC) (p. 29)

9. Sketch of cat on
flaked limestone;
Egyptian artist's
trialpiece, late New
Kingdom (1580–1100
BC) (p. 29)

10. Bronze figure of Bast, the
Egyptian cat-headed Goddess
(663–30 BC)

11. Egyptian bronze cat

12. Egyptian bronze cat
('Gayer-Anderson cat') with
gold earrings and nose-ring

13. Cat herding geese; satirical wall painting of animals in procession. Egypt, New Kingdom (p. 36)

14. The Great Cat Ra killing Aapep the serpent; Papyrus of Hunefer XIXth Dynasty (*circa* 1300 BC) (p. 43 and p. 92)

15. Bird seized by cat; mosaic, Rome

16. Cat stalking a pheasant; Hagia Triada fresco, Crete (*circa* 1600 BC) (p. 30)

the honourable title '*Der Katzen Raphael*' and his drawings and paintings were eagerly collected even by reigning sovereigns. Visitors observed that his favourite cat Minette was always near him when at work; 'and he seemed' (says an article in the *Penny Magazine* of 1 March 1834) 'to carry on a sort of conversation with her by gestures and by words. Sometimes this cat occupied his lap, while two or three kittens were perched on each shoulder, or reposed in the hollow formed at the back of his neck, while sitting in a stooping posture at his table'.

This description of Mind at work with his cats is reminiscent of another, and earlier, cat-lover, John Rich the actor. In an account of Peg Woffington's first introduction to Rich, Augusta Daly describes how she was astounded to find him surrounded by twenty-seven cats, one of whom was lapping the cream for his tea and two were reposing on his knees; another was asleep on his shoulder while a fourth sat demurely on his head!

It was during Mind's life that the Swiss authorities detected symptoms of madness among the cats of Berne in the year 1809 and ordered the destruction of 800. Mind managed to secrete and save his own Minette but it is said that he never got over the tragedy of the execution of so many cats.

Another artist who produced many cat drawings was Théophile Alexandre Steinlen who was born in Lausanne in 1859; he went to Paris as a young man where, like so many artists, he suffered extreme poverty. At length in a little café called *Au Chat Noir*, he met the '*chansonniers*' Bruant and Jules Jouy, whose work he illustrated. His drawings appeared chiefly in journals, among them *Le Chat Noir*. One of his cartoons, published in a collection by Chatto and Windus in 1911, is entitled *Metamorphosis* and depicts a horrific scene of witches mounting broomsticks while an excited pack of cats on the roof urges them on.

Many of his drawings of cats have great charm and he was much in demand by advertisers. He also illustrated menus and invitations such as *Diner du Bon-bock* and *Diner du Petit Cochon*.

Both Steinlen and Mind drew the natural cat in many attitudes, poses and activities. Wain, on the other hand, enjoyed chiefly depicting cats behaving comically as humans. Despite this less serious view of the art, Wain's twentieth-century cats are quite equal to those of Mind and Steinlen (illust 75).

Comparable with these artists in brilliance of presentation of cats are the Japanese artists Utamaro (who lived in the late eighteenth century and died in 1806) and Kuniyoshi (1798–1861). Utamaro's 'Cat's Dream' (illust 54) was painted, according to S. Bing in *Artistic Japan*, by way of a rest from the great artist's more serious work. Bing points out that in Japan dreams come not from the brain but from the heart (or, as Edmond de Goncourt observed, from the stomach). For this reason the bubble of smoke in which the dream is wrapped comes from the throat.

Kuniyoshi, who was born in 1798, was as a child called Yoshizō or

Yoshisaburō and in later life Ikusa Magosaburō. It was not until about 1814 when he finished his apprenticeship that he was given the professional name of Kuniyoshi. By 1830 he had become established as a print-designer of the first rank. Many of his prints were theatrical illustrations, among them a triptych of 1835 and that reproduced in illust 61 and 62 of the famous actor Onoye Kikugorō in 1847 when he again took the part of the horrific cat-witch of Okabe in a play of the various traditions and stories of the fifty-three post stations of the Tōkaidō road.

In his book on Kuniyoshi, based mainly on his own and the Victoria and Albert Museum's collections, B. W. Robinson, Deputy Keeper of the Department of Metal Work, writes:

During this period [1842–1846], too, Kuniyoshi's prints of women, children, and comic subjects are as numerous as ever, and in many of the former cats are introduced. Kuniyoshi's love of cats impressed his contemporaries and has intrigued subsequent collectors of his prints. One of his earliest cats, about 1830, appears on a *surimono* in the series *Fūzoku onna Suikoden*: a girl is reclining with a pipe and a book, keeping her legs warm under a coverlet which also covers the brazier, or *hibachi,* and on the resulting erection is a splendid tiger-like creature with arched back, glaring at his mistress. But it is in the years about 1840 that Kuniyoshi's cats appear most frequently. We have heroic stories, scenes of everyday life [illust 59], and theatrical productions all represented by cats; there are actors caricatured as cats [illust 63], cats forming the *kana* characters for the names of fish, and in unnumbered prints of women at their domestic occupations cats appear, sleeping, fawning, playing with their kittens, stealing fish, washing themselves, or playing with a ball or the trailing tail of a *kimono*. In all these Kuniyoshi demonstrates his wonderfully sympathetic understanding of feline nature. Kyōsai, who became his pupil as quite a young boy, has left a hilarious sketch in his *Kyōsai gwadan* of the uproarious scene which was apparently normal in Kuniyoshi's studio; the master presides benignly, a cat in the bosom of his *kimono,* while his pupils bicker, everything is in confusion, and there are cats all over the place. In each of his self-portraits (and he has left at least five, all, alas, from the back) Kuniyoshi has included one of his cats, and in his memorial portrait by Yoshitomi he is represented holding a tobacco-pouch with a *netsuke* formed of a group of cats. In the later censorship period (1847–52) Kuniyoshi produced a series of proverbs illustrated by cats, and a wonderful triptych with a cat or group of cats for each of the fifty-three stations of the Tōkaidō road. Needless to say, his original drawings include many studies of his cats, mostly rapid sketches in which he has unerringly caught the complete relaxation of a cat asleep, its characteristic attitude with upthrust hind-leg as it performs its intimate toilet, and many other poses and expressions which all cat-lovers will recognize with delight.

One of the most charming of Kuniyoshi's prints in Mr Robinson's collection, but not mentioned above, is reproduced at illust 55. This depicts a cat chasing a butterfly which has just been painted by the daughter of Dainagon Yukinari and which is so realistic that the cat imagines it to be alive.

Ancient Greece has provided us with few paintings or sculptures of cats. The most celebrated is the pictorial relief which, with two others, decorated three sides of a square block of marble, discovered in 1922, which was built into the ancient city-wall of Athens. Like two other blocks, it was the pedestal of a statue and a relic of the period before the Persian destruction of Athens in 480 B.C. In the scene (illust 18) two youths are inciting a cat and dog to fight, while other young men stand by to watch. In his book *Classical Sculpture*, A. W. Lawrence points out that 'the vermilion background survives in two of the sculptured sides of the older base . . . ; the ground-work of the figures seems to have been polished instead of painted, though details were picked out in colours, such as the red on the crown worn by the youth in charge of the cat. Here appears a great similarity of idea to contemporary vases, in which figures of the natural colour of the pot were contrasted with a black background. The resemblance to vase painting is indeed overwhelming and indicates that the artist earned his living more by this method than by sculpture: the date suggested by a comparison with the paintings of such men as Euthymides is the last ten or fifteen years of the sixth century.' The sculptured panel is one foot in height.

On a vase or lekythos which was found in 1916 in a pit by the sea shore, not far from Taranto, in the South of Italy, a woman is depicted sheltering under an umbrella or parasol, while a youth opposite her holds a cat crouching on his arm. Between them, two cupids are wrestling (illust 17). The vase is believed to have been the work of an Attic artist who had settled in Apulia, probably in Taranto itself, about the end of the fourth century B.C. – that is, about 200 years later than the Athenian relief. Archaeologists infer from the umbrella, the struggling cupids and the cat, that the vase could not have been made in Attica itself, where the cat was little known and the other devices not known at all.

Other vases of similar design have been discovered in Southern Italy on which cats crouch on the forearm of a standing or leaning figure. In one of these a cat is shown endeavouring to catch a bird which is being held by a youth.

Pottery and porcelain, particularly in modern times, provide a large number of cats. Many of these have a humorous aspect, such as the two seventeenth-century Lambeth Delft cats on illust 86. In some we meet again the topsy-turvy world of Brueghel's painting, of the grotesques of church architecture and of the marginal decorations in many mediaeval manuscripts. There is for example in the Fitzwilliam Museum in Cambridge a large round blue and white plate (illust 51) on which an owl, a monkey and a cat appear dressed up, with the following rhyme:

The alomode or ye maidens mode admir'd continu'd
by ye ape, owl & mistris puss   1688

I heare ye clamors of ye Thron
Wherein they would run top knots down
But yet alas, alas al in vain
For I this mode will still maintain.

I am ye owl, yt stood in feare
Of other birds. It doth appeare
But being in this dresse I'll vow
I don't beleeve they'l know me now.

Top knots & night railes I declare
For evermore I meane to ware
This dresse there's no ye can excell
I see it doth becom me well.

How, now you females of this age
I would not have you in a Rage
Although I doe present you heare
With what you have esteeme Deare
Top knots & night rails you odore
But see by whom they now are wore.

Ye cat shee weares in perfect view
A cornet & a top knot too
Ye very owl that flyes by night
In this your mode takes mouch delight
Ye reasons this for in a storm
This rail will keep her shoulders warm.

Ye very ape odores this dress
& cryes it up. Can we do less
But females ye first found this pride
Pray tell mee how can you abide
To weare this mode against controul
When used by ape, nay cat and owl.

This is no new conceit, as from earliest times, animals have been portrayed engaged in various activities normally performed by human beings.
In a mural from ancient Egypt, now in the British Museum, the cat is
shown herding geese (illust 13).

It has been suggested that to a people who believed in the transmigration of souls it was natural that animals should be represented per-
forming tasks carried out by men before their reincarnation, and that as
the cat was regarded as the messenger or guider of souls to the under-
world, it was particularly appropriate in its case. While this may be true

of the examples which have come down to us from ancient Egypt, the many mediaeval carvings in cathedrals* and churches to be found in the United Kingdom and on the Continent of the same type of subject are probably deliberate skits or lampoons of current types or practices. Perhaps the clearest examples of this are the carvings or paintings of a cat (or other animal) playing the fiddle (or other musical instrument), indicating that the artist regarded the noise produced by, say, the fiddle or trumpet as little better than caterwauling or the braying of donkeys (see illust 50); the resemblance of the large-eared cat playing the fiddle on the carving in Hereford Cathedral (illust 28) suggests that the carver had in mind, even if he was not directly copying, a manuscript like Queen Mary's Psalter.

Some of the suggested derivations of the phrase 'cat and fiddle' are set out in the essay on inn signs (page 145ff). It is significant, however, that the phrase was apparently sufficiently well known by the fourteenth century, when the carvings on the tip-up seats, or misericords, in the choirs in Wells and Hereford cathedrals were produced, to have caught the imagination of the carvers, and to have conjured up a picture of a cat playing the fiddle or other instrument. The fiddle is also the instrument played in a scene on a bench-end in Fawsley church, where the carvings date from the first half of the sixteenth century, and were executed by the Knyghtley family. Another church cat and fiddle, now very difficult to distinguish, is to be found in the porch of the parish church at Northleach, Gloucestershire. On a poppyhead in the choir at Farthingstone, Northamptonshire, it is the panpipes on which a cat plays to lure forth two mice from under the stool. A cat plays the single pipe in a spandrel near the high altar of Lichfield Cathedral.

A possible survival of Isis worship has been suggested for the carving in the left hand 'supporter' to a 'cat' misericord dating from 1530 in Beverley Minster, where the cat plays the fiddle to four kittens; the instrument connected with the worship of both Isis and her daughter, the cat-headed Bast, was the sistrum, which also had four strings, and the repetition of the number '4' has been thought to signify the number of weeks in the month and therefore refers to the moon goddess. As Tindall Wildridge points out, the moon means 'measurer' and the cat is playing a dance measure.

The position of the cat in ancient Egypt has been very fully dealt with in a number of books published during the last century; in a book concerned with the cat in art one can only touch very briefly on certain of the aspects of the history of the cat in religion, in order to explain the pieces of sculpture or painting that have come down to us. There is often

* Many of the animal carvings in churches and cathedrals appear on misericords. These are hinged seats, mostly in choir stalls, and the carvings are on the under-surface. The seats were originally designed to relieve aged priests who, having to stand throughout the services, could rest, without appearing to sit, on the ledges on the under-surface while the seat itself was in the vertical position.

confusion between the true cat goddess, Bast or Bastet, worshipped at Bubastis, and the lion-headed goddess, Sekhmet, who embodied the more savage aspects of the sun. Bastet is to be found on a papyrus leading a soul to Osiris, king of the dead, but in Egypt, it was often the other way round, and the goddess Amenti escorted to Paradise the souls of cats, grasping their paws, and helping them up the ladder until Horus and Set could pull them up. In Babylon the welfare of a holy man's soul was entrusted to a cat and the Malayan tribe, the Jakuns, thought of the cat as the one which led men through hell to paradise, reducing the temperature by spraying water. The cat undertook a similar duty in Finnish folklore.

Cats have also been worshipped, or at any rate connected with religious observance, in Babylon, Burma, Siam and Japan. A New York collection of musical instruments contains a Japanese instrument in the shape of a cat, which was used to produce a rattling sound at certain points in their temple services by scraping the cat's spine with a stick; a character cut on its forehead signifying 'pleasure' was also struck.

In England, the cat's own pleasure in music, even when not the performer, is suggested in the parish church at Gresford, Denbigh, on a misericord where two cats are engaged in a stately dance to the music of a pig playing the bagpipes (illust 32). (The pig has unfortunately disappeared, except for a faint outline only discernible by the initiated, by means of the remaining portion of a trotter.) On the large poppyhead in the nave at Farthingstone (illust 27) a cat sits on the shoulder of a winged jester (himself a cat) who plays the drum. The cat is also found on the shoulder of a jester-drummer in Holdenby Church, Northants, on a misericord believed to have come originally from Lincoln; cats play an unwilling part in providing the music at Boston, where jesters bite their tails to make them yell. One could even quote as further evidence of the cats' delight in music the remains of a painting in the Maison des Templiers at Metz, where a cat holds a hymn book while, in company with a sow, it listens to Reynard preach, an ass and a unicorn providing the music.

A different aspect of the topsy-turvy world can be seen in illust 46, which is one of a series at the foot of Harleian MS 6563, illustrating battles between cats and rats, with stones and crossbow; sometimes the cats and sometimes, as here, the rats are in the tower. The turning of the tables by the rats is found in legend and has survived pictorially in many countries, including Egypt, Persia, Japan and Russia. In a misericord at Great Malvern Priory (illust 40) the mice are shown hanging the cat, while two owls (also rat-catchers) look on. On the abacus of a capital in Tarragon Cathedral, Spain, there is a series of carvings, the main scene of which shows a cat being borne on a stretcher to execution, with the rat as executioner bearing an axe, but in the sequel, reminiscent of the tale of Raminagrobis and of the cat in Aesop's fable who hung himself up, the cat springs on the rat and their fortunes are again reversed. An exquisite carving of the rats attempting to bell the cat is in the Parish Church at Kempen on the Rhine. The cat is shown caught in a familiar attitude with paw uplifted (illust 34) – an attitude common in many restaurants in Far Eastern countries with the sign of the 'Beckoning Cat'.

In Bristol Cathedral, Tybert appears in three scenes illustrating the popular mediaeval romance of Reynard the Fox, from which an extract is given on pages 79–82; on two misericords the cat is attacking the priest and on the third (illust 39) he helps to hang Reynard. The same scene appears in a manuscript now in the Bodleian Library.

The majority of cats carved in wood or stone in cathedrals or churches in England do not appear to have any special significance but to be straightforward representations of the animal as known to the carvers; they are usually shown catching mice or rats, though occasionally carrying a kitten; the best example of the mother cat is probably that at Upper Sheringham, Norfolk, on an arm-rest (illust 41); the head has been rubbed smooth by many hands, which gives the cat a somewhat bald look, but the concentration and the delicate hold on the back of the kitten's neck are faithfully recorded. There is a very worn poppyhead of the same subject at South Lopham in Suffolk, and at Woolpit in the same county on a sixteenth-century arm-rest an animal which, from the anxious expression, one would guess to be a cat forced to move her kitten, is carved at one end of a bench, and a fierce cat holding a rat's head in its mouth at the other. (One could, however, take this 'mother cat' for a dog, as it has an unusually bulging forehead. It is often difficult to determine for certain what animal is intended from the rather worn wood carvings we see in churches, particularly in East Anglia; carvings at Stowlangtoft, Tuttington, etc., bear this out. The large cat-like animal fighting with a man in armour in Exeter Cathedral (illust 33) is no doubt intended to be one of the larger cat tribe.

The cat's role as hunter impressed itself on man from earliest times and in this capacity he, or she, is shown on Norman fonts at Hodnet, Salop and at Kirkburn, Yorkshire; even in the twentieth century, Tommy the cat is remembered in Exeter Cathedral; his carved head is in the chapel of St James and St Thomas, restored after the Second World War. The rat with which he was engaged when he was attacked by an owl and lost one eye is represented in the opposite corner, while the carver has put his own portrait to the right of the window in the same chapel. At Lichfield, the cat is given pride of place, appearing over the bishop's seat in the chapter house; he is a fierce tom cat, which has just pounced on a mouse (illust 7). The cat's role as a destroyer of vermin was no mean one in the Middle Ages, as, indeed, today.

The cat appears with a mouse at Winchester, Godmanchester and several times at Beverley; the centre of the misericord which has the fiddle-playing cat to the left is reproduced in illust 5, and the right supporter, on which a kitten examines a large mouse with interest as if it were a toy, is given in illust 36. (Miss Emma Phipson in her *Choir Stalls and their Carvings* refers to the main scene as being a cat encouraging her kitten to chase a rat, but as the 'kitten' and rat are identical, it would appear that this is a 'two-rat' cat.) The more normal savage tearing of prey is shown on an arm-rest at Boston, and a very worn example is found on the exterior of the church at Haversham, Buckinghamshire. One of the more unusual of these carvings is that of a kitten on top of a mousetrap, from which it has just taken a mouse, at North Cadbury in Somerset (illust 2). The loftiest carved wooden cat is probably that in a very dark oak spandrel in the Lady Chapel of the magnificent parish church in Cirencester, in Gloucestershire. Here a portly cat is sitting up while a rat or large mouse is shown rushing towards her, its tail well up into the upper angle of the spandrel.

There are also attractive carvings of a cat sitting bolt upright with its tail curled over its back in Wordwell church in Suffolk, a fifteenth-century carving (from which half the cat's head has been cut away) having been copied in the nineteenth century. A cat's head peers out between leaves on the capital of a pillar in the chapter house at York. The cat on the cornice at Marlborough commemorates the bravery of the church cat in saving her kittens from a fire.

A cat appears in a cosy domestic scene at Ripple, Worcestershire, where it is washing its paw, seated behind the old woman who, with her husband, sits over the fire in the scene representing February. This could serve to illustrate Burns' lines in 'Sic a wife as Willie had':

> Auld Baudrons by the ingle sits,
>   An' wi' her loof her face a-washin':
> But Willie's wife is nae sae trig,
>   She dights her grunzie wi' a hushion.

The paw behind the ears, in the familiar face-washing attitude, is portrayed on an arm-rest in the stalls of Great Malvern Priory.

The dressed-up cat appears on the south side of the cornice at Evercreech (illust 6), but here a healthy scorn for human clothes is shown by the kitten who endeavours to tear off the cloak from his girl-friend.

The term 'cat's head' (or more commonly 'beak-head') is of course well known as a form of decoration used over arches in Norman and Romanesque architecture; the heads often have little resemblance to a cat apart from two ears. There are, however, a number of heads, mostly of early date, which may or may not be intended as true cats. A number of these heads, including those at Pot Shrigley and Cranleigh, Surrey, are reputed to have inspired Lewis Carroll for his famous Cheshire Cat. Tenniel's cat head has been reproduced in the Carroll commemorative window at Daresbury, though it has less resemblance to the original than has the Mock Turtle in the same window. A Cheshire cat, but this time

17. Vase with a girl watching two cupids wrestling while a young man holds her cat on his arm. Southern Italy (400–300 BC) (p. 35)

18. Cat and dog fight, on Attic relief (*circa* 500 BC) (p. 35)

19. Adam and Eve with cat and other animals; the 'Fall of Man', engraving by
Albrecht Dürer (1504) (p. 30)

20. Virgin and Child with cat; drawing by Leonardo da Vinci (p. 30)

21. Virgin and Child with cat, and Joseph at the window; etching by Rembrandt (1654) (p. 30)

22. 'Belling the cat' in the painting of Netherlandish Proverbs by Peter Brueghel
the Elder (1559) (p. 31)

23. Don Manuel Osorio de Zuñiga with his cats; painting by Goya

Le vray portrait du chat du grand Duc de Moscouie
_.1663._

24. Portrait of the Grand Duke of Moscovy's cat; engraving by Wenceslaus
Hollar (1663) (p. 32)

25. Cat receiving a deputation of mice or rats; engraving by Wenceslaus Hollar

26. The Graham children's cat, from the painting by Hogarth (1742) (p. 32)

complete and elongated, appears on the tower at Grappenhall. The subject of one of the tapestry seat cushions in Gloucester Cathedral is Dick Whittington and his cat (referring to the legend that he came from Pauntley Court in Gloucestershire). A more famous embroidery cat, with a mouse or rat, is that which hangs in Mary Queen of Scots' own bedroom in Holyrood in Edinburgh. It is said that this cat, embroidered by Mary herself, symbolized Elizabeth who played with her, as a cat with a mouse.

Occasionally the cat comes to church in connection with a local family; the wild cat which crouches at the feet of Sir Percival Cresacre in Barnburgh church, in the West Riding, is part of the memorial to the knight, attacked by a wild cat with whom he fought for some three miles until they both died of their wounds in the church porch. There is also a cat with a mouse in its mouth lying in the attitude normally adopted by dogs, at the feet of a worn figure at Old Cleeve, Somerset, whose history is now lost. A collared cat appears on a bench-end at St Austell, Cornwall. The head of a cat with a rat in its mouth is the emblem of the Dawson family, and is seen on the village fountain at Hornby, Lancashire. One of the most charming of such 'family' cats is the cream-coloured marble cat crouching at the feet of its master in Wing church in Buckinghamshire. This cat is covered with black spots, rather like the cats on Egyptian wall-paintings.

Apart from the mouse or rat, the animal with which the cat is probably most commonly connected is the dog; the cat and dog appear on one of several misericords of cats which the carver at Wells left unfinished. On the painted wooden roof of St Mary's church at Bury St Edmunds, a black terrier dog has just sprung on a white cat, which is obviously yelling for help. It has gained the mastery, however, on a boss in the college Chantry at Winchester, where it rides on the dog, blowing a horn, with a stick and a rat over its shoulder. Cat and dog sit in apparent amity (though here the dog is howling) on either side of an old hag with a distaff on a misericord in St Mary's church, Minster-in-Thanet. An old woman is shown with a cat, presumably meant to be sitting on her lap, on the corbel table at Saffron Walden. More interesting is the carving at Winchester seen in illust 37. Here the old woman is apparently actually riding on the cat, and a reference may be intended to a witch riding off to a coven, although the distaff and the bobbin which she holds are normal symbols of the female sex and have no special connection with witches. (It is a monkey that rides on the cat on the cornice at Bloxham and on another misericord at Beverley (illust 35).)

Representations of witches are usually on rather horrible broadsheets or other illustrations, and cats appear in some of these either as domestic familiars or as the form taken by the witches themselves. These were probably the mediaeval equivalent of the modern horror comic. The horrific character is only redeemed if there is beauty of design and execution, as in Kuniyoshi's drawings of the Okabe witch-cat. The forked tail of the dancing cat in illust 61 was one of the signs of the cat-demon, and in it lay some of its powers of bewitching. It is interesting to compare a cat with a double tail on the capital of the French church at Canterbury, though here the extra tail may be merely intended as decoration. Double-tailed cats are, of course, found in Irish legend and the idea may have been in the carver's mind.

Anyone who has studied the subject will have been struck by the fact that the cat which had been worshipped and pampered in ancient Egypt was tortured and reviled, burnt alive and harried in mediaeval times. The contrast is not, of course, pure chance, or a natural restoring of balance, as the depths to which it had sunk in the popular estimation, and the dread it evoked as the supposed familiar or shape taken by a witch or devil, were the direct consequence of its earlier high favour, the later religion being forced by the persistence of survivals of the earlier religions to stamp them out and represent them as wholly evil.

The cat is possibly intended to represent evil on the seventeenth-century tiles from Barcelona now in Womersley church, Yorkshire, when it appears in a scene of the Last Supper. There was a convention that the cat appeared at the feet of Judas, and it is so shown by Cellini, Luini and Ghirlandaio. The symbolism of the cat as traitor is a fairly easy extension of its use by the Romans, the Swiss, Dutch, French and many others as a symbol of liberty and thus of free thinking. It was also shown at the feet of the Pope to signify perfidy and hypocrisy in a volume entitled *Les Crimes des Papes*.

The cat has, however, also been connected with several saints, including St Agatha, who was known as St Gato in the old province of Languedoc.

St Gertrude of Nivelles, the patroness of cats, gardeners, travellers and widows, was said to be invoked not only by souls in purgatory, but by anyone who might be alarmed or plagued by mice; she is sometimes depicted accompanied by a cat as well as, more commonly, by mice or rats.

St Jerome is sometimes shown with a domestic cat (instead of, or even as well as, his lion), the cat being the companion of philosophers; there is an example in Antonello de Messina's picture in the National Gallery; and there is a children's poem which runs:

> If I lost my little cat, I should be sad without it,
> I should ask St Jerome what to do about it,
> I should ask St Jerome, just because of that
> He's the only Saint I know that kept a pussy-cat.

St Yves of Treguier, in Brittany, is also connected with cats – in fact, he is sometimes shown as one. The St Yves' cat is symbolic of all the evil qualities attributed to lawyers (of whom he is the patron saint), as like them, the cat watches for his opportunity, falls on his victims and never lets them go; which may have something to do with Rabelais' creation, *Les Chats-Fourrés*.

In Italian legend, a cat saved St Francis from a plague of mice by magically springing from his sleeve; while in Irish legend, St Moling reproved his cat for springing on a swallow, which had in its turn eaten a fly; in obedience to the Saint's command, both swallow and fly were restored. St Cadoc, the Welsh prince who became an anchorite, seems to have been less well disposed towards cats, as he is occasionally shown giving the cat to the Devil on the bridge. The place of the Saint is taken by the Lord Mayor of Beaugency on the Loire in a tale told by James Joyce in a letter to his grandson Stephen. In return for their fine new bridge, the Devil had bargained to take the first person who crossed it; the Mayor made sure that this person was a cat, by carrying it on to the bridge and then pouring a bucket of water over it to drive it towards the waiting Devil. In a more gentle scene, in modern glass at Brockle-hampton in Herefordshire another Saint, St Cecilia, is shown with a cat and kittens at her feet.

Possibly due to its long connection with Isis, Diana and other virgin goddesses, the cat has also been connected with the Holy Family and is so shown in the painting by Baroccio (in the National Gallery) as well as by Rembrandt and Leonardo da Vinci (illust 21 and 20). There is an Italian legend that a cat was suckling her kittens in the stable when Jesus was born – this cat is usually shown with a cross on its back.

The cat is sometimes regarded as poised midway between good and evil, as the being that knew both, when it is portrayed with Adam and Eve in the Garden of Eden; it is interesting to compare the place of the Great Cat, Ra, who killed the serpent of darkness, Aapep, hard by the Persea Tree, also a tree of life and knowledge. Apart from Dürer's representation of this subject referred to above, it has been portrayed by Franz Floris and Jan Brueghel, with a cat at the foot of the tree, and is also found in some old stained glass inside the tower at Haslemere, in Surrey.

It is not only in enmity that the cat and snake have been linked; in Japan the cat and the serpent were said to be the only two creatures who failed to weep for Buddha's death. In Egyptian and other mythologies, the coiled snake and the cat curled into a circle were both thought of as symbols of eternity, having no beginning and no end, and containing both good and evil. The identification of the cat with the serpent is exemplified by the Norse myth in which Thor attempted to lift the cat but was unable to move more than one paw from the ground and found that in fact he was struggling with the Midgaard Serpent which encircled the earth.

The identification of two such different creatures is natural enough even in the matter of fact terms of today, for everyone can appreciate the singular mystery and grace which pertain to both.

Mediaeval views on cats

On the Nature of Cats

The cat in youth is a full lecherous beast. He is swyft plyant and merry. He leapeth and clymbeth on eurything that is before hym. He is led by a straw and playeth therewith and is a right heauy beste in age, and full slepy and lieth slyly in wait for mice, and is aware where they be more by smell than by sight and hunteth and pounceth upon them in priuy places. And when he takyth a mous he playeth therewith and eteth hym after the play. There be hard fyghting for wyues. They mak a ruthful noise and ghastful when one proffereth to fyght with another. . . . And when he hath a fair skin he is as it were proud thereof and goeth fast about: but when his skin is burnt, then he abydeth at home. And is oft for his fair skin taken by the skinner and slain and flayed.

from *De Proprietatibus Rerum* by Bartolomeus Anglicus (thirteenth century), tr. by John de Trevisa 1397

Of the Cat

The Cat in Latin is called *Catus*, as if you woulde say *Cautus*, warie or wise.

In Greeke she is named *Galiootes,* with the Germaines *Kaiz*. She is to the Mouse a continuall enimie: verie like to the Lyon in tooth and clawe: and useth to pastime or play with the Mouse ere she deuoureth hir. She is in hir trade and maner of liuing very shamefast: always louing clenlinesse. There is also a kinde thereof called the wild Cat, which of all things is annoyed with the smell of Rue, and the Almond leafe, and is driuen away with that sooner then with any other thing.

from *A Greene Forest,* or a naturall Historie . . . .
compiled by John Maplet, M. of Arte and student in Cambridge:
entending hereby that God might especially be glorified;
and the people furdered. 1567

The Musion

The beaste is called a Musion, for that he is enimie to Myse, and Rattes. And he is called a Catte of the Greekes because he is slye, and wittie: for that he seeth so shaepely, that he overcommeth darkness of the nighte, by the shyninge lyghte of his eyne. In shape of body he is like unto a Leoparde, and hath a greate mouth. He dothe delighte that he enjoyeth his libertie: and in his youthe he is swifte, plyante, and merye. He maketh a rufull noyse, and a gastefull, when one profereth to fighte with an other. He is a cruell beaste, when he is wilde, and falleth his owne feete from moste highe places: and oneth is hurte therewith. When he hathe a fayre skinne (he is, as it were, prowde thereof), and then he goeth faste aboute to be seene.

from *Workes of Armorie*, by Bossewell, 1572

Of the Cat

A Cat is a familiar and well known beast, called of the Hebrews, *Catull,* and *Schanar,* and *Schundra*; of the Grecians, *Aeluros,* and *Kattes,* and *Katis*; of the Saracens, *Katt*; the Italians, *Gatta,* and *Gotto*; the Spaniards, *Gata,* and *Gato*; the French, *Chat*; the Germans, *Katz*; the Illyrians, *Kozka,* and *Furioz* (which is used for a Cat by Albertus Magnus) and I conjecture, to be either the Persian or the Arabian word. The Latins call it *Feles,* and sometimes *Murilegus,* and *Musio,* because it catcheth Mise, but most commonly *Catus,* which is derived of *Cautus,* signifying wary. Ovid saith, that when the Giants warred with the Gods, the Gods put upon them the shapes of Beasts, and the sister of Apollo lay for a spy in the likeness of a Cat, for a Cat is a watchful and wary beast seldom overtaken, and most attendant to her sport and prey: according to that observation of Mantuan;

Of the name

The nature and etymology of a Cat

> Non secus ac muricatus, ille invadere pernam,
> Nititur, hic rimas oculis observat acutis.

And for this cause did the Egyptians place them for hallowed beasts, and kept them in their Temples, although they alleadged the use of their skins for the cover of Shields, which was but an unreasonable shift, for the softness of a Cats skin is not fit to defend or bear a blow: It is known also, that it was capital among them, to kill an Ibis, an Aspe, a

Their use among the Egyptians

Crocodile, a Dog, or a Cat; in so much as, that in the dayes of King Ptolemie, when a peace was lately made betwixt the Romans and the Egyptians; and the Roman Ambassadors remaining still in Egypt, it fortuned that a Roman unawares killed a Cat, which being by the multitude of the Egyptians espied, they presently fell upon the Ambassadors house, to rase down the same, except the offender might be delivered unto them to suffer death: so that neither the honour of the Roman name, nor the necessity of peace, could have restrained them from that fury, had not the King himself and his greatest Lords come in person not so much to deliver the Roman Cat-murderer, as to safeguard him from the peoples violence. And not only the Egyptians were fools in this kind, but the Arabians also, who worshipped a Cat for a God; and when the Cat dyed, they mourned as much for her, as for the father of the family, shaving the hair from their eyelids, and carrying the beast to the Temple, where the Priests salted it and gave it a holy funeral in Bubastum, (which was a burying place for Cats neer the Altar) wherein may appear to all men, in what miserable blindness the wisest men of the world, (forsaking, or deprived of the true knowledge of God) are more then captivated so that their wretched estate cannot better be expressed then by the words of St Paul, When they thought to be wise, they became fools.

Once Cats were all wild, but afterward they retired to houses, wherefore there are plenty of them in all Countries: Martial in an Epigram celebrated a Pannonian Cat with this distichon;

Pannonicas nobis nunquam dedit Umbria Cattas,
Mavult haec dominae mittere dona pudens.

The Spanish black Cats are of most price among the Germans; because they are nimblest, and have the softest hair fit for garment.

A Cat is in all parts like a Lioness, except in her sharp ears, wherefore the Poets feign, that when Venus had turned a Cat into a beautiful woman, (calling her *Aeluros*) who forgetting her good turn, contended with the Goddesse for beauty; in indignation whereof, she returned her to her first nature, only making her outward shape to resemble a Lion; which is not altogether idle, but may admonish the wisest, that fair and foul, men and beasts, hold nothing by their own worth and benefit, but by the virtue of their

A History

Caelius

Of the taming of Cats and their countries

The best Cats

Creator: Wherefore if at any time they rise against their maker, let them think to lose their honour and dignity in their best part, and to return to baseness and inglorious contempt; out of which they were first taken, and howsoever their outward shape and condition please them, yet at the best are but beasts that perish, for the Lions suffer hunger.

Cats are of divers colours, but for the most part griseld, like to congealed ise, which cometh from the condition of her meat: her head is like unto the head of a Lion, except in her sharp ears: her flesh is soft and smooth: her eyes glister above measure, especially when a man cometh to see them on the suddain, and in the night they can hardly be endured, for their flaming aspect. Wherefore Democritus describing the Persian Smaragde saith that it is not transparent, but filleth the eye with pleasant brightness, such as is in the eyes of Panthers and Cats, for they cast forth beams in the shadow and darkness, but in sunshine they have no such clearness, and thereof Alexander Aphrodise giveth this reason, both for the sight of Cats and Bats, that they have by nature a most sharpe spirit of seeing.

Sipontius
of the several parts

Albertus compareth their eye-sight to Carbuncles in dark places, because in the night they can see perfectly to kill Rats and Mice: the root of the herb Valerian (commonly called *Phu*) is very like to the eye of a Cat, and wheresoever it groweth, if Cats come thereunto, they instantly dig it up, for the love thereof, as I my self have seen in mine own Garden, and not once only, but often, even then when as I had caused it to be hedged or compassed round about with thornes, for it smelleth marvellous like to a Cat.

The Egyptians have observed in the eyes of a Cat, the encrease of the Moon-light, for with the Moon they skin more fully at the full, and more dimly in the change and wane, and the male Cat doth also vary his eyes with the Sun; for when the Sun ariseth, the apple of his eye is long; toward noon it is round, and at the evening it cannot be seen at all, but the whole eye sheweth alike.

Gillius

The tongue of a Cat is very attractive and forcible like a file, attenuating by licking the flesh of a man, for which cause, when she is come neer to the bloud, so that her own spittle be mingled therewith, she falleth mad. Her teeth are like a saw, and if the long hairs growing about her mouth (which some call Granons) be cut away, she loseth her courage. Her nails sheathed like the nails of a Lion, striking with her forefeet, both Dogs and other things, as a man doth with his hand.

Pliny

47

This beast is wonderful nimble, setting upon her prey like
a Lion, by leaping, and therefore she hunteth both Rats, all
kind of Mice, and Birds, eating not only them, but also fish,
where withall she is best pleased. Having taken a Mouse, she
first playeth with it, and then devoureth it, but her watchful
eye is most strange, to see with what pace and soft steps, she
taketh birds and flies; and her nature is to hide her own
dung or excrement, for she knoweth that the savour and
presence thereof, will drive away her sport, the little Mouse
being able by that stool, to smell the presence of her mortal
foe.

To keep Cats from hunting of Hens, they use to tie a little
wilde Rew under their wings, and so likewise from Dove-
coates, if they set it in the windowes, they dare not approach
unto it for some secret in nature. Some have said that Cats
will fight with Serpents, and Toads, and kill them, and perceiving that she is hurt by them; she presently drinketh
water and is cured: but I cannot consent unto this opinion:
it being true of the Weasell as shall be afterward declared.

Pontzettus sheweth by experience that Cats and Serpents
love one another, for there was (saith he) in a certain
Monastery, a Cat nourished by the Monkes, and suddenly
the most parts of the Monks which used to play with the
Cat fell sick: whereof the Physitians could find no cause, but
some secret poison, and all of them were assured that they
never tasted any: at the last a poor labouring man came unto
them, affirming that he saw the Abbey-cat playing with a
Serpent, which the Physitians understanding, presently con-
ceived that the Serpent had emptied some of her poison
upon the Cat, which brought the same to the Monks, and
they by stroking and handling the Cat, were infected therewith; and whereas there remained one difficulty, namely,
how it came to passe, the Cat her self was not poisoned
thereby, it was resolved, that for as much as the Serpents
poison came from him but in play and sport, and not in
malice and wrath, that therefore the venom thereof being
lost in play, neither harmed the Cat at all, nor much en-
dangered the Monks: and the very like is observed of Mice
that will play with Serpents.

Cats will also hunt Apes, and follow them to the woods,
for in Egypt certain Cats set upon an Ape, who presently
took himself to his heels, and climed into a tree, after whom
the Cats followed with the same celerity and agility: (for
they can fasten their clawes to the barke and run up very
speedily:) the Ape seeing himself overmatched with number

27. Cat-jester with a cat on his shoulder; poppyhead, Farthingstone Church, Northamptonshire (p. 38)

28. A duet between a goat playing a lute and a cat playing a fiddle; misericord, Hereford Cathedral (p. 37)

29. Cat playing a fiddle; misericord, Wells Cathedral (p. 37)

30. Cat playing a fiddle for kittens to dance; misericord, Beverley Minster

31. Cat playing a fiddle to kittens; bench-end, Fawsley Church, Northamptonshire (p. 37)

32. Two cats dancing to the piping of a pig; misericord (mutilated), Gresford Church, Denbigh (p. 38)

33. Knight and cat fighting; misericord, Exeter Cathedral (p. 39)

of his adversaries, leaped from branch to branch, and at last took hold of the top of a bough, whereupon he did hang so ingeniously, that the Cats durst not approach unto him for fear of falling, and so departed.

The nature of this beast is, to love the place of her breeding, neither will she tarry in any strange place, although carryed far, being never willing to forsake the house, for the love of any man, and most contrary to the nature of a Dog, who will travaile abroad with his master; and although their masters forsake their houses, yet will not these beasts bear them company, and being carried forth in close baskets or sacks, they will yet return again or lose themselves. A Cat is much delighted to play with her image in a glasse, and if at any time she behold it in water, presently she leapeth down into the water which naturally she doth abhor, but if she be not quickly pulled forth and dryed she dyeth thereof, because she is impatient of all wet. Those which will keep their Cats within doors, and from hunting birds abroad, must cut off their ears for they cannot endure to have drops of rain distill into them, and therefore keep themselves in harbour. Nothing is more contrary to the nature of a Cat, then is wet and water, and for this cause came the proverb that they love not to wet their feet. It is a neat and cleanly creature, oftentimes licking her own body to keep it neat and fair, having naturally a flexible back for this purpose, and washing her face with her forefeet: but some observe, that if she put her feet beyond the crown of her head, that it is a presage of rain, and if the back of a Cat be thin the beast is of no courage or valew. They love fire and warm places, whereby it often falleth out that they often burn their Coats. They desire to lie soft, and in the time of their lust (commonly called cat-wralling) they are wilde and fierce, especially the males, who at that time (except they be gelded) will not keep the house: at which time they have a peculiar direful voice. The manner of their copulation is this, the female lyeth down, and the male standeth, and their females are above measure desirous of procreation, for which cause they provoke the male, and if he yeeld not to their lust, they beat and claw him, but it is only for love of young, and not for lust: the male is most libidinous, and therefore seeing the female will never more engender with him during the time her young ones suck, he killeth and eateth them if he meet with them, (to provoke the female to copulation with him again, for when she is deprived of her young, she seeketh out the male of her own accord) for which the

The love of home

Albertus.
A way to make Cats keep home

A conjectural secret

Their copulation

Aristotle

female most warily keepeth them from his sight. During the time of copulation, the female continually cryeth, whereof the Writers give a double cause; one, because she is pinched with the talons or clawes of the male in the time of his lustful rage; and the other, because his seed is so fiery hot, that it almost burneth the females place of conception. When they have littered, or as we commonly say kittened, they rage against Dogs, and will suffer none to come neer their young ones. The best to keep are such as are littered in March; they go with young fifty daies, and the females live not above six or seven years, the males live longer, especially if they be gelt or libbed: the reason of their short life is their ravening of meat which corrupteth within them.

They cannot abide the savour of ointments, but fall mad thereby; they are sometimes infected with the falling evill, but are cured with Gobium. It is needless to spend any time about her loving nature to man, how she flattereth by rubbing her skin against ones Legs, how she whurleth with her voice, having as many tunes as turnes, for she hath one voice to beg and to complain, another to testifie her delight and pleasure, another among her own kind by flattering, by hissing, by puffing, by spitting, in so much as some have thought that they have a peculiar intelligible language among themselves. Therefore how she beggeth, playeth, leapeth, looketh, catcheth, tosseth with her foot, riseth up to strings held over her head, sometimes creeping, sometimes lying on the back, playing with one foot, sometime on the belly, snatching now with mouth, and anon with foot, apprehending greedily anything save the hand of a man, with divers such gestical actions, it is needless to stand upon; in so much as Caelius was wont to say, that being free from his Studies and more urgent weighty affaires, he was not ashamed to play and sport himself with his Cat, and verily it may well be called an idle mans pastime. As this beast hath been familiarly nourished of many, so have they payed dear for their love, being requited with the losse of their health, and sometime of their life for their friendship: and worthily, because they which love any beast in a high measure, have so much the lesse charity unto man.

Therefore it must be considered what harmes and perils come unto men by this beast. It is most certain, that the breath and savour of Cats consume the radical humour and destroy the lungs, and therefore they which keep their Cats with them in their beds have the air corrupted, and fall into severall Hecticks and Consumptions. There was a certain company of Munks much given to nourish and play with Cats, whereby they were so infected, that within a short space none of them were able either to say, read, pray, or sing, in all the Monastery; and therefore also they are dangerous in the time of pestilence, for they are not only apt to bring home venemous infection, but to poison a man with very looking upon him; wherefore there is in some men a natural dislike and abhorring of Cats, their natures being so composed, that not only when they see them, but being neer them and unseen, and hid of purpose, they fall into passions, frettings, sweating, pulling off their hats and trembling fearfully, as I have known many in Germany; the reason whereof is, because the constellation which threatneth their bodies which is peculiar to every man, worketh by the presence and offence of these creatures: and therefore they have cryed out to take away the Cats.

The like may be said of the flesh of Cats, which can seldom be free from poison, by reason of their daily food, eating Rats and Mice, Wrens and other birds which feed on poison, and above all the brain of a Cat is most venomous, for it being above measure dry, stoppeth the animal spirits, that they cannot passe into the ventricle, by reason whereof memory faileth, and the infected person falleth into a Phrenzie. The cure whereof may be this, take of the water of sweet Marjoram with *Terra lemnia* the weight of a groat mingled together, and drink it twice in a month, putting good store of spices into all your meat to recreate the spirits withall, let him drink pure Wine, wherein put the seed of *Diamoschu*. But a Cat doth as much harm with her venemous teeth, therefore to cure her biting, they prescribe a good diet, sometime taking Hony, Turpentine, and Oil of Roses melt together and laid to the wound with *Centory*; sometime they wash the wound with the urine of a man, and lay to it the brains of some other beast and pure Wine mingled both together.

Of a Cats flesh

Ponzettus
Alexander

The hair also of a Cat being eaten unawares, stoppeth the Artery and causeth Suffocation: and I have heard that when a childe hath gotten the hair of a Cat into his mouth, it hath so cloven and stuck to the place that it could not be gotten off again, and hath in that place bred either the wens or the Kings evill. To conclude this point, it appeareth that this is a dangerous beast, and that therefore as for necessity we are constrained to nourish them for the suppressing of small vermine: so with a wary and discreet eye we must avoid their harms, making more account of their use then of their persons.

Mathaeolus

In Spain and Gallia Narbon, they eat Cats, but first of all take away their head and tail, and hang the prepared flesh a night or two in the open cold air, to exhale the savour and poison of it, finding the flesh thereof to be almost as sweet as a Cony. It must needs be an unclean and impure beast that liveth only upon vermin and by ravening, for it is commonly said of a man when he neeseth, that he hath eaten with Cats; likewise the familiars of Witches do most ordinarily appear in the shape of Cats, which is an argument that this beast is dangerous to soul and body. It is said that if bread be made wherein the dung of Cats is mixed, it will

Perottus

drive away Rats and Mice. But we conclude the story of this beast with the medicinal observations, and tarry no longer in the breath of such a creature compounded of good and evill. It is reported that the flesh of Cats salted and sweetened hath power in it to draw wens from the body, and being warmed to cure the Hemorrhoids and pains in the reins and back, according to the Verse of Ursinus

Et lumbus lumbis praestat adesus opem

Galenus
The medicina virtues of a Cat

Aylsius prescribeth a fat Cat sod for the Gowt, first taking the fat, and anointing therewith the sick part, and then wetting Wool or Tow in the same, and binding it to the offended place.

For the pain and blindness in the eye, by reason of any skins, webs, or nails, this is an approved medicine; Take the head of a black Cat, which hath not a spot of another colour in it, and burn it to powder in an earthen pot leaded or glazed within, then take this powder and through a quill blow it thrice a day into thy eye, and if in the night time any heat do thereby annoy thee, take two leaves of an Oke wet in cold water and bind them to the eye, and so shall all pain

Galen

flie away, and blindness depart although it hath oppressed thee a whole year: and this medicine is approved by many Physicians both elder and later.

The liver of a Cat dryed and beat to powder is good against the stone: the dung of a female Cat with the claw of an Oul hanged about the neck of a man that hath had seven fits of a Quartain Ague, cureth the same: a neesing powder made of the gall of a black Cat and the weight of a groat thereof taken and mingled with four crowns weight of Zambach, helpeth the convulsion and wryness of the mouth:

Sextus
Aetius
Rasis
Albertus
Pliny

and if the gall of a Cat with the black dung of the same Cat, be burned in perfume under a woman travelling with a dead childe, it will cause it presently to come forth: and Pliny saith that if a pin, or thorn, or fishbone, stick in ones mouth, let him rub the outside against it with a little Cats dung, and it will easily come forth. Given to a woman suffering the flux, with a little Rozen and Oil of Roses, it stayeth the humour; and for a web in the eye of an horse, evening and morning blow in the powder of Cats dung, and it shall be cured.

from *The History of Four-footed Beasts* by Edward Topsell

The Diminutive Lyon or Catus, *the Cat*

I. It is called in Hebrew, בטול, מחנד, *Catul, Schanar,* in *Chaldean,* חתול, *pl.* חתולין, *Chatul, pl. Chatulin;* in Greek, Κατλης, αἰλυρος; in Latin, *Catus, felis;* in English; *the Cat,* but the wild Cat is supposed to be called in Hebrew, איים, *Jim. Isa.* 13, 22, and 34, 14. for so *Arius Montanus* translates it; as for *Kat* or *Cat,* it is the most usual name that almost all Nations call it by.*

II. It is bred and is an Inhabitant of almost all Countries in the World, all *Cats* were at first wild, but were at length tamed by the industry of Mankind; it is a Beast of prey, even the tame one, more especially the wild, it being in the opinion of many nothing but a diminutive Lyon.

III. It is now said to be of three kinds, 1. *The tame Cat.* 2. *The wild wood Cat.* 3. *The Cat of Mountain,* all which are of one nature, and agree much in one Shape, save as to their magnitude, the *wild Cat* being larger much than the Tame, and the *Cat of Mountain* much larger than the *wild Cat.*

IV. It has a broad Face almost like a Lyon, short Ears, large Whiskers, shining Eyes, short smooth Hair, long Tail, rough Tongue, and armed on its Feet with Claws, being a crafty, subtle watchful Creature, very loving and familiar with Man-kind, the mortal enemy to the Rat, Mouse, and all sorts of Birds, which it seizes on as its prey. As to its Eyes, Authors say that they shine in the Night, and see better at the full, and more dimly at the change of the Moon; as also that the Cat doth vary his Eyes with the Sun, the Apple of its Eye being long at Sun rise, round towards Noon, and not to be seen at all at night, but the whole Eye shining in the night. These appearances of the Cats Eyes I am sure are true, but whether they answer to the times of the day, I never observed.

* This follows original text but more correctly should read: 'It is called in Hebrew חתול, שונר, Chatul, Shunar; in Aramaic חתול, pl. חתולין, Chatul, Chatulin; .... the Wild Cat is believed to be called in Hebrew איים, Iyyim, Isa. 13, 22 and 34, 14....'

V.   It is a neat and cleanly creature, often licking it self, to keep it fair and clean, and washing its Face with its fore-feet; the best are such as are of a fair and large kind, and of an exquisite Tabby color, called *Cyprus* Cats. They usually generate in the winter Season, making a great noise, go 56 Days or 8 weeks with young, and bring forth 2, 3, 4, 5, 6, or more at a time, they cover their excrements, and love to keep their old habitations.

VI.   *Its Flesh* is not usually eaten, yet in some Countries it is accounted an excellent Dish, but the Brain is said to be poisonous, causing madness, stupidity, and loss of memory, which is cured only by vomiting, and taking musk in Wine. The Flesh applied easeth the pain of Hæmorrhoids and the back, and salted, beaten, and applied, draws Thorns, &c. out of the Flesh, and is said particularly to help the Gout, especially that of the wild Cat.

VII.   *The Fat* is hot, dry, emollient, discussive, and Anodyne: R⁊ *Cat's Grease,* ℥ij. *Palm Oyl,* ℥β. *Oil of Anniseed,* ℈j. *mix them*; it dissolves tumors, eases pain, and prevails against nodes in the Shin, and the cold Gout.

VIII.   *The Head:* R⁊ *the Ashes of a Cat's Head* ℥j. *white vitriol in fine Pouder,* Saccharum Saturni *ana* ℈j. *mix them for a Pouder*; or mix them with Honey for a Balsam, blown into the Eyes, or annointed thrice aday; it cures Blindness, and most Diseases of the Eyes, as the Pin and Web, Pearls, Clouds, Films, &c.

IX.   *The Liver:* R⁊ *the Ashes, or rather pouder of it,* ℥j. *Borax, Nitre, Volatile Sal Armoniack, Pouder of Elecampane, Roots of Bay-berries,* ana ℈j. *mix them.* Dose ℈ij. in any convenient Vehicle, against Gravel and stoppage of Urine.

X.   *The Gall:* R⁊ *of Cat's Gall,* ℥β. *of our* Aqua Regulata ℈ij. *Honey,* ℈j. *mix them for a* Collyrium to wash the Eyes often with against Pearls, Films, Blindness, and Dimness of the sight: R⁊ *Cat's Gall* ℥β. Colo quintida, *fine Aloes, ana* q. s. *Musk gr.* xvi. *mix and make a pessary.* It brings away the birth and after birth, and extracts a Mola.

XI.   *The Blood,* some affirms it kills Worms in the Nose, and other places of the Skin: R⁊ *the Bloud of the Tail of a Bore-Cat* gut. x. *Salt of Man's Skull, gr.* vj. *pouder of Ox horns,* gr. 10. *mix them for a Dose.* It is said to cure the Falling-Sickness.

XII.   *The Dung and Urine:* R⁊ *Pouder of Cats Dung,* ℥j. *Mustard-seed in Pouder,* ℈iij. *Juice of Onions,* ℈ii. *Bears Grease enough to make an Oyntment.* It cures Baldness and the Alopecia.

from *The English Physician,* or The Druggist's Shop Opened
by William Salmon

Arsinoë's cats

Imitation of the manner of the later Greek Poets, *circa* A.D. 500.
Cats were unknown in historic Greece till about the Christian era.

Arsinoë the fair, the amber-tressed,
   Is mine no more;
Cold as the unsunned snows are is her breast,
   And closed her door.
No more her ivory feet and tresses braided
   Make glad mine eyes;
Snapt are my viol strings, my flowers are faded;
   My love-lamp dies.

Yet, once, for dewy myrtle-buds and roses,
   All summer long,
We searched the twilight-haunted garden closes
   With jest and song.
Ay, all is over now – my heart hath changed
   Its heaven for hell;
And that ill chance which all our love estranged
   Is this wise fell:

A little lion, small and dainty sweet
   (For such there be!)
With sea-grey eyes and softly stepping feet,
   She prayed of me.
For this, through lands Egyptian far away
   She bade me pass;
But, in an evil hour, I said her nay –
   And now, alas!
Far-travelled Nicias hath wooed and won Arsinoë
With gifts of furry creatures white and dun
   From over-sea.

from *Concerning Cats*, by Graham R. Tomson

To Pangur Ban, my White Cat

Pangur Ban was written in Irish by an Irish monk at Reichenau and is the second of four poems in a commonplace book, the manuscript Codex Sancti Pauli, preserved in the monastery of St Paul and dating from the ninth century. From the days when St Patrick, the son of a Roman-British landowner, went as Bishop of Ireland in the fifth century, monastic houses and foundations sprang up and flourished and from them Irish scholars, philosophers and poets wandered all over Europe. It is to one of these exiles that we owe the charm and freshness of Pangur Ban. The translation, by the late Samuel Courtauld, is in the same metre as the original poem.

Brother artists, he and I
Special crafts elect to ply;
Hunting mice would Pangur choose:
I have different sporting views.

At my books I never tire,
Nor rewards of fame desire:
Proud of inborn talents he
Never thinks of envying me.

Snug indoors who roam abroad?
By ourselves we're never bored:
Countless thrilling tests arise
For our keenest faculties.

He, superbly dexterous,
Many a time entraps the mouse:
Truth elusive I pursue –
Sometimes I can trap her too!

Pangur's pupils, full and bright,
Fix the wainscot in their sight:
Through the walls of science I
Seek with feebler shafts to pry.

Pangur glories in his skill
When his claws achieve a kill:
I am overjoyed to gain
Prizes hunted in the brain.

Thus we live from day to day,
Neither in the other's way,
And our pleasures win apart,
Following each his special art.

Perfect use of eye and limb
Daily practice gives to him:
I my task appointed find
Chasing darkness from the mind.

Mice before milk

Lat take a cat and fostre hym wel with milk
And tendre flessch and make his couche of silk,
And lat hym seen a mouse go by the wal,
Anon he weyvith milk and flessch and al,
And every deyntee that is in that hous,
Suich appetit he hath to ete a mous.

from *The Manciple's Tale*, by Geoffrey Chaucer

The mouse's escape

In come Gib Hunter, our jolly cat,
And bade 'God Speed'. The Burges up with that
And to the hole she went as fire from flint.
Bawdrons the other by the back has hint.
From foot to foot he cast her to and fro,
Whiles up, whiles down, as cant as any kid;
Whiles would he let her run under the straw;
Whiles would he wink and play with her butshid;
Thus to the silly Mouse great pain he did,
While at the last through fortune and good hap
Betwixt ane boarde and the wall she crap.

from *The Burges Mouse and the Uplandis Mouse*,
by Robert Henryson (1425 ?-1500 ?)

Nico the shepherd's cat

I have (and long shall have) a white great nimble cat,
A king upon a mouse, a strong foe to the rat,
Fine eares, long taile he hath, with Lions curbed clawe,
Which oft he lifteth up, and stayes his lifted pawe,
Deepe musing to himselfe, which after-mewing showes,
Till with lickt beard, his eye of fire espie his foes.

from Nico and Dorus, in the *Second Eclogues of Arcadia*
by Sir Philip Sidney, 1554-1586

The lover

Whose Mistresse feared a mouse

If I might alter kind,
    What, think you, I would bee?
Nor Fish, nor Foule, nor Fle, nor Frog,
    Nor Squirril on the Tree;
The Fish the Hooke, the Foule
    The lymed Twig doth catch,
The Fle the Finger, and the Frog
    The Bustard doth dispatch.

The Squirril thinking nought,
    That feately cracks the Nut,
The greedie Goshawke wanting pray
    In dread of Death doth put;
But scorning all these kindes,
    I would become a Cat,
To combat with the creeping Mouse,
    And scratch the screeking Rat.

I would be present, aye,
    And at my Ladie's call;
To gard her from the fearfull Mouse,
    In Parlour and in Hall;
In Kitchen, for his Lyfe,
    He should not shew his head;
The Peare in Poke should lie untoucht
    When shee were gone to Bed.
The Mouse should stand in Feare,
    So should the squeaking Rat;
And this would I do if I were
    Converted to a Cat.

George Turberville (1540–1610)

Cat into lady

A certain Young Man used to play with a beautiful Cat, of which he grew so fond, that at last he fell in love with it to such a degree, that he could rest neither night nor day for the excess of his passion. In this condition he prayed to Venus, the goddess of beauty, to pity and relieve his pain. The good-natured goddess was propitious, and heard his prayers; and the Cat, which he held in his arms, was instantly transformed into a beautiful Young Woman. The Youth was transported with joy, and married her that very day. At night, while they were in bed, the bride unfortunately heard a mouse behind the hangings, and sprang from the arms of her lover to pursue it; the Youth was ashamed, and Venus offended, to see her sacred rites thus profaned by such unbecoming behaviour; and perceiving that her new convert, though a woman in outward appearance, was a Cat in her heart, she caused her to return to her old form again, that her manners and person might be suitable to each other.

Application

This Fable, however extravagant and unnatural in its composition, is intended to depicture and check the blind instinctive ardour of the passion of love, the transports of which cover all imperfections, so that its devotees consider neither quality nor merit. It is like an idol of our own creating, which we fashion into whatever figure or shape we please, and then run mad for it. The Fable also shows that

'No charm can raise from dirt a grov'ling mind';

And that people of a low turn of spirit and mean education cannot change their principles by changing their situation: for in the midst of splendour and magnificence, they still retain the same narrow sentiments, and seldom fail to betray, by some dirty action, their original baseness, which no embroidery can conceal; and though fortune has been pleased to lift them out of the mire, we still see the silly awkward blockheads displaying their lack of mind and education through all their ensigns of dignity. If any thing more need be added, it can only be with a view of more plainly putting inexperienced youth on their guard against making inconsiderate connections, lest they take a Cat into their bosom, instead of an amiable consort and companion for life.

from Aesop's *Fables,* illustrated by Thomas Bewick (1818)

The ratcatcher and cats

The rats by night such mischief did,
Betty was ev'ry morning chid:
They undermin'd whole sides of bacon,
Her cheese was sapp'd, her tarts were taken,
Her pasties, fenc'd with thickest paste,
Were all demolish'd and laid waste.
She curst the cat for want of duty,
Who left her foes a constant booty.
    An Engineer, of noted skill,
Engag'd to stop the growing ill.
    From room to room he now surveys
Their haunts, their works, their secret ways.
Finds where they 'scape an ambuscade,
And whence the nightly sally's made.
    An envious Cat, from place to place,
Unseen, attends his silent pace,
She saw that if his trade went on,
The purring race must be undone,
So, secretly removes his baits,
And ev'ry stratagem defeats.
    Again he sets the poison'd toils,
And puss again the labour foils.
    What foe (to frustrate my designs)
My schemes thus nightly undermines?
Incens'd, he cries: this very hour
The wretch shall bleed beneath my power.
    So said. A pond'rous trap he brought,
And in the fact poor puss was caught.
    Smuggler, says he, thou shalt be made
A victim to our loss of trade.
    The captive Cat with piteous mews
For pardon, life and freedom sues.
A sister of the science spare,
One int'rest is our common care.
    What insolence! the man reply'd,
Shall cats with us the game divide?
Were all your interloping band
Extinguish'd, or expell'd the land,

We Rat-catchers might raise our fees,
Sole guardians of a nation's cheese!
   A Cat, who saw the lifted knife,
Thus spoke, and sav'd her sister's life.
   In ev'ry age and clime we see,
Two of a trade can ne'er agree,
Each hates his neighbour for encroaching;
Squire stigmatizes squire for poaching;
Beauties with beauties are in arms,
And scandal pelts each other's charms;
Kings too their neighbour kings dethrone,
In hope to make the world their own.
But let us limit our desires,
Not war like beauties, kings and squires,
For though we both one prey pursue,
There's game enough for us and you.

from *Fables*, by John Gay, 1733

The old woman and her cats

Who friendship with a knave hath made
Is judg'd a partner in the trade.
The matron, who conducts abroad
A willing nymph, is thought a bawd;
And if a modest girl is seen
With one who cures a lover's spleen,
We guess her, not extremely nice,
And only wish to know her price.
'Tis thus, that on the choice of friends
Our good or evil name depends.

A wrinkled hag, of wicked fame,
Beside a little smoky flame

Sat hov'ring, pinch'd with age and frost;
Her shrivell'd hands, with veins embost,
Upon her knees her weight sustains,
While palsy shook her crazy brains;
She mumbles forth her backward prayers,
An untam'd scold of fourscore years.
About her swarm'd a num'rous brood
Of Cats, who lank with hunger mew'd.

Teaz'd with their cries her choler grew,
And thus she sputter'd. Hence, ye crew.
Fool that I was, to entertain
Such imps, such fiends, a hellish train!
Had ye been never hous'd and nurst
I, for a witch, had ne'er been curst.
To you I owe, that crouds of boys
Worry me with eternal noise;
Straws laid across my pace retard,
The horse-shoe's nail'd (each threshold's guard)
The stunted broom the wenches hide,
For fear that I should up and ride;
They stick with pins my bleeding seat,
And bid me shew my secret teat.

To hear you prate would vex a saint,
Who hath most reason of complaint?
Replies a Cat. Let's come to proof.
Had we ne'er starved beneath your roof,
We had, like others of our race,
In credit liv'd, as beasts of chace.
'Tis infamy to serve a hag;
Cats are thought imps, her broom a nag;
And boys against our lives combine,
Because, 'tis said, your cats have nine.

from *Fables*, by John Gay

34. Rats planning to bell the cat; misericord, Kempen Parish Church, Rhineland (p. 39)

35. Monkey combing
a cat; misericord,
Beverley Minster
(p. 41)

36. Cat playing with
a mouse; misericord,
Beverley Minster
(p. 39)

37. Old woman riding
on a cat; misericord,
Winchester Cathedral
(p. 41)

38. *Opposite page:*
Tybert the cat clawing
naked Priest;
misericord, Bristol
Cathedral (p. 39)

39. Tybert helping to
hang Reynard the Fox;
misericord, Bristol
Cathedral (p. 39)

40. Mice hanging a cat;
misericord, Great
Malvern Priory (p. 38)

41. Cat with kitten;
bench-end, Upper
Sheringham Church,
Norfolk (p. 39)

42. Cat with kitten;
bench-end, Woolpit
Church, Suffolk (p. 39)

The witch

'Dear friends next door, forgive me this intrusion!
I warn you that a witch can cause confusion
By magically altering her form
Into a beast, to do us men much harm.

Your cat's my wife! Indeed, I am awake!
I'm absolutely sure! I can't mistake
Her scent, her sidelong look, her claws,
Her noisy purr, the way she licks her paws.'

The neighbour and his wife cried out in fear –
'Take back the hussy, we don't want her here!'
Their watch-dog barked and made a frightful row,
But puss, quite unperturbed, said gently, 'Miaow!'

after *Die Hexe,* by Heinrich Heine

Raminagrobis, or the cat judge

One day a lady weasel seized the home
Of a young rabbit who'd gone out to roam.
'Twas but a cunning trick the house to seize,
But master being out, a thing of ease.
So weasel brought her Household Gods to stay
What time our rabbit had just gone away
To pay his devoir to the rosy dawn
Amid the dew and thyme upon the lawn.
Now when he'd grazed and scampered here and there,
Back hurried Johnnie Rabbit to his lair.
'Ye Gods! What do I see? Am I quite sane?
Dame Weasel's nose pressed close against the pane!'
And loud he cried, 'My father's house in pawn!

Here! Madam Weasel! Ere the trumpet sounds,
Evacuate my home; you're out of bounds;
Or else I'll call upon the regiment
Of rats, who all this countryside frequent'.

Replied the lady of the pointed nose:
'To her who takes it first, possession falls;
Ah, what a *casus belli* for two foes,
A dwelling into which the owner crawls!
And even if it were a realm,' said she,
'I'd really like to know what statute old
Has made the grant of properties freehold –
Perhaps to John, the son, descends the key.
Has Peter's nephew claims? or Will's? I'm told
They have more claim than Paul or even me!'

John Rabbit urged both custom and old use;
'These laws,' said he, 'this house gave me alone.
They made me master, me, my father's son;
To Peter first, then Simon, then me, John.
The first arrival! What a lame excuse!'
'Well, well,' said Madam, 'Say no more! To Puss,
Raminagrobis, then let's put our case.'
This Cat a holy hermit's life enjoyed.

In truth demure, with holy life he toyed;
A holy man, he had a cat's own face,
Luxuriant fur and size and plumpy grace,
A skilful referee on any case.

To him as Judge, Jack Rabbit did agree
And there and then each claimant made a plea
Before His Royal Furry Majesty.
The Cat whom some call Grippeminaud, with glee
Remarked: 'Approach, my dears, this deaf old cat.'
Without alarm they came towards his mat.
When Grippeminaud, the sanctimonious knave,
Saw them within his reach, he bared his claws;
He seized his prey whom wisdom could not save
And made the two agree within his jaws.

from *Fables*, by La Fontaine

The cat and the mice

A certain house being much infested with Mice, a Cat was at length procured, who very diligently hunted after them, and killed great numbers every night. The Mice, being exceedingly alarmed at this destruction among their family, consulted together upon what was best to be done for their preservation against so terrible and cruel an enemy. After some debate, they came to the resolution, that no one should, in future, descend below the uppermost shelf. The Cat, observing their extreme caution, endeavoured to draw them down to their old haunts by stratagem, for which purpose, she suspended herself by her hinder legs upon a peg in the pantry, and hoped by this trick to lull their suspicions, and to entice them to venture within her reach. She had not long been in this posture, before a cunning old Mouse peeped over the edge of the shelf, and squeaked out thus: Aha! Mrs Puss, are you there then? There may you be; but I would not trust myself with you, though your skin were stuffed with straw.

Application

We cannot be too much upon our guard against fraud and imposition of every kind; and prudence in many cases would rather counsel us to forego some advantages, than endeavour to gain them at a risk of which we cannot certainly ascertain the amount. We should more particularly suspect some design in the professions of those who have once injured us; and though they may promise fairly for the future, it is no breach of charity to doubt their sincerity, and decline their proposals, however plausible they may appear; for experience shews that many of the misfortunes which we experience through life, are caused by our own too great credulity.

from Aesop's *Fables*, illustrated by Thomas Bewick

My cat Jeoffry

While confined in Bedlam, where his companion was his cat Jeoffry, Smart wrote a long and strange poem

Rejoice in the Lamb
A Song from Bedlam

For I will consider my cat Jeoffry.
For he is the servant of the living God, duly and daily serving him.
For at the first glance of the glory of God in the East he worships in his way.
For is this done by wreathing his body seven times round with elegant quickness.
For then he leaps up to catch the musk, which is the blessing of God upon his prayer.
For he rolls upon prank to work it in.
For having done duty and received blessing he begins to consider himself.
For this he performs in ten degrees.
For first he looks upon his fore-paws to see if they are clean.
For secondly he kicks up behind to clear away there.
For thirdly he works it upon stretch with the fore-paws extended.
For fourthly he sharpens his paws by wood.
For fifthly he washes himself.
For sixthly he rolls upon wash.
For seventhly he fleas himself, that he may not be interrupted upon the beat.
For eighthly he rubs himself against a post.
For ninthly he looks up for his instructions.
For tenthly he goes in quest of food.
For having consider'd God and himself he will consider his neighbour.
For if he meets another cat he will kiss her in kindness.
For when he takes his prey he plays with it to give it a chance.
For one mouse in seven escapes by his dallying.
For when his day's work is done his business more properly begins.
For he keeps the Lord's watch in the night against the adversary.
For he counteracts the powers of darkness by his electrical skin and glaring eyes.
For he counteracts the Devil, who is death, by brisking about the life.

For in his morning orisons he loves the sun and the sun loves him.

For he is of the tribe of Tiger.

For the Cherub Cat is a term of the Angel Tiger.

For he has the subtlety and hissing of a serpent, which in goodness he suppresses.

For he will not do destruction, if he is well-fed, neither will he spit without provocation.

For he purrs in thankfulness, when God tells him he's a good Cat.

For he is an instrument for the children to learn benevolence upon.

For every house is incompleat without him & a blessing is lacking in the spirit.

For the Lord commanded Moses concerning the cats at the departure of the Children of Israel from Egypt.

For every family had one cat at least in the bag.

For the English cats are the best in Europe.

For he is the cleanest in the use of his fore-paws of any quadrupeds.

For the dexterity of his defence is an instance of the love of God to him exceedingly.

For he is the quickest to his mark of any creature.

For he is tenacious of his point.

For he is a mixture of gravity and waggery.

For he knows that God is his Saviour.

For there is nothing sweeter than his peace when at rest.

For there is nothing brisker than his life when in motion.

For he is of the Lord's poor and so indeed is he called by benevolence perpetually – Poor Jeoffry! poor Jeoffry! the rat has bit thy throat.

For I bless the name of the Lord Jesus that Jeoffry is better.

For the divine spirit comes about his body to sustain it in compleat cat.

For his tongue is exceeding pure so that it has in purity what it wants in musick.

For he is docile and can learn certain things.

For he can set up with gravity which is patience upon approbation.

For he can fetch and carry, which is patience in employment.

For he can jump over a stick which is patience upon proof positive.

For he can spraggle upon waggle at the word of command.

For he can jump from an eminence into his master's bosom.

For he can catch the cork and toss it again.

For he is hated by the hypocrite and miser.

For the former is afraid of detection.

For the latter refused the charge.

For he camels his back to bear the first motion of business.

For he is good to think on, if a man would express himself neatly.

For he made a great figure in Egypt for his signal services.

For he killed the Icneumon-rat very pernicious by land.

For his ears are so acute that they sting again.

For from this proceeds the passing quickness of his attention.
For by stroaking of him I have found out electricity.
For I perceived God's light about him both wax and fire.
For the Electrical fire is the spiritual substance, which God sends from
  heaven to sustain the bodies both of man and beast.
For God has blessed him in the variety of his movements.
For, tho he cannot fly, he is an excellent clamberer.
For his motions upon the face of the earth are more than other quadrupeds.
For he can tread to all the measures upon the musick.
For he can swim for life.
For he can creep.

from *Jubilate Agno*, by Christopher Smart (1722–71)

Doctor Johnson and his cat

CAT: a domestick animal that catches mice, commonly reckoned by naturalists the lowest order of the leonine species. Johnson's *Dictionary*

The Doctor's biographer, James Boswell, disliked cats, but he does not record ever having confessed as much to the Doctor himself.

'I shall never forget', he wrote, 'the indulgence with which he treated Hodge, his cat, for whom he himself used to go out and buy oysters lest the servants, having that trouble, should take a dislike to the poor creature. . . .

'I am unluckily one of those who have an antipathy to a cat, so that I am uneasy when in the room with one; and, I own, I frequently suffered a good deal from the presence of this same Hodge. I recollect him one day scrambling up Dr Johnson's breast, apparently with much satisfaction, while my friend, smiling and half whistling, rubbed down his back and pulled him by the tail.'

Yet, for all his antipathy, Boswell remarked that 'it was a fine cat'.

' "Why, yes, Sir," (said the Doctor), "but I have had cats whom I have liked better than this"; and then, as if perceiving Hodge to be out of countenance; he added "but he is a very fine cat, a very fine cat indeed." '

On another occasion, when talking of a certain young gentleman of 'Good Family', the Doctor declared:

' "Sir, when I heard of him last, he was running about town shooting cats." And then, in a sort of kindly reverie, he bethought himself of his own favourite cat and said, "But Hodge shan't be shot; no, no, Hodge shall not be shot." '

43. Cats and a mouse in thirteenth-century Bestiary, Harl. Ms. 4751

44. Monkey forcing a cat to snatch chestnuts from the fire; seventeenth-century Dutch stained-glass roundel in window of Bowes Museum, Barnard Castle

45. Cat with mouse; Luttrell Psalter
46. Cat with crossbow attacks rats' castle; 15th century Book of the Hours,
Harl. Ms. 6563

47. *Opposite page:* Cat playing fiddle; Harl. Ms. 6563
48. Cat playing bagpipes; Harl. Ms. 6563
49. Cat with mouse in mouth playing zither; Harl. Ms. 6563
50. Cat playing tabor and donkey playing trumpet; Queen Mary's Psalter

51. Lambeth Delft plate with a satirical design showing a cat, an owl and a monkey dressed up (1688) (p. 35 and p. 36)

Madame Paillan's pension

An imaginary conversation:

CARDINAL RICHELIEU: It is my desire, my dear Abbé, to do something to make life easier for Madame Marie de Gournay. I fear that I mocked her cruelly over her pamphlet advocating the preservation of ancient words and terms in the French language. She told me that I was laughing at a poor old woman. She said that I expected everyone to 'contribute to my diversion'. I feel that I deserved her rebuke and should like to show my contrition by making an *amende honorable*. After all, she is an educated woman and was the friend of Montaigne.

ABBÉ DE BOISROBERT: I am delighted to hear Your Eminence say so. What do you wish me to do?

CARDINAL RICHELIEU: I should like her to have a pension of two hundred crowns.

ABBÉ DE BOISROBERT: Hm! Has Your Eminence remembered that Madame de Gournay has to keep a man-servant?

CARDINAL RICHELIEU: Well, let him have fifty.

ABBÉ DE BOISROBERT: And Madame Paillan?

CARDINAL RICHELIEU: And who is Madame Paillan?

ABBÉ DE BOISROBERT: Her cat, Your Eminence. What about her? In the name of Your Eminence's own cats, Moussard le Fougueux, Racan, Soumise and Ludovic le Cruel, what about Madame Paillan?

CARDINAL RICHELIEU: Let Madame Paillan have twenty crowns – er – on condition that she has kittens.

ABBÉ DE BOISROBERT: Oh, my dear friend, Madame Paillan has *had* kittens!

CARDINAL RICHELIEU: Another *pistole*, then!

Sir Roger de Coverley and Moll White

This account raised my curiosity so far that I begged my friend Sir Roger to go with me into her hovel, which stood in a solitary corner under the side of the wood. Upon our first entering Sir Roger winked to me and pointed at something that stood behind the door, which, upon looking that way I discovered to be an old broomstaff. At the same time he whispered me in the ear, to take notice of a tabby cat that sat in the chimney-corner, which, as the old knight told me, lay under as bad a report as Moll White herself, for besides that Moll was said often to accompany her in the same shape, the cat is reported to have spoken twice or thrice in her life and to have played several pranks above the capacity of an ordinary cat.

extract from paper No. 117 contributed to *The Spectator* by Joseph Addison (1711)

Misailury

'*Some that are mad if they behold a cat*' Shakespeare

From hence they passed to eels, then to parsnips, and then from one aversion to another, until we had worked ourselves up to such a pitch of complaisance, that when the dinner was to come in we enquired the name of every dish, and hoped that it would be of no offence to any of the company, before it was admitted. When we had sat down, this civility among us turned the discourse from eatables to other sorts of aversions; and the eternal cat, which plagues every conversation of this nature, began then to engross the subject. One had sweated at the sight of it, another had smelled it out as it lay concealed in a very distant cupboard; and he who crowned the whole set of these stories, reckoned up the number of times in which it had occasioned him to swoon away. 'At last,' sayd he, 'that you may all be satisfied of my invincible aversion to a cat, I shall give an unanswerable instance: As I was going through a street of London, where I never had been until then, I felt a general damp and faintness all over me, which I could not tell how to account for, until I chanced to cast my eyes upwards, and found that I was passing under a sign-post on which the picture of a cat was hung.'

from *The Spectator*, No. 538, 17 November 1712

The unwelcome cat

The world contains no other person who
Detests the Cat as fiercely as I do;
Its eyes, its brows, its steady stare I hate
And when it comes too near I'm in a state;
I dash away, my nerves all jangling wire;
No cat shall come to share my bedroom fire!
And I detest those silly people who
Can't live at home without a cat, don't you?
And when I stay with them their dreadful cat,
Instead of lying still upon the mat,
Invades my room and puts himself to bed
Upon my feather pillow near my head!
The side I'm used to lie on is my left;
Of sleep I'm then by Cock alone bereft.
But now the miaowing cat makes such a din
I'm jerked awake and jump from out my skin;
I call the servants, turning heels o'er head;
Comes John and lights a candle by my bed,
While Thomas swears I am a lucky wight
To have a visit from a cat that's white.
Says James, 'A single cat appears to show
A night of pain at last is on the go!'

after *Le Chat,* by Pierre de Ronsard (1524–85)

Maykittens

Kittens born in May are traditionally believed to bring ill luck. One Celtic theory is that they cause snakes to come into the house and that they should not therefore be allowed to survive – which conflicts with the Egyptian doctrine of the enmity between the Great Cat Ra and the serpent Aapep.

Some believe that Maykittens make troublesome ill-behaved cats and an old Huntingdonshire proverb supports this view:

> May chets
> Bad luck begets
> And sure to make dirty cats.

That Maykittens, if not properly controlled, may cause troublesome problems, is pleasantly suggested in the poem 'Von Katzen' by Theodor Woldsen Storm (1817–88), of which a free translation appears below:

Maykittens

It was the first of May, my charming little cat
Deposited six lovely kittens on the mat,
All white, Maykittens, each with miniature black tail –
Oh, what a lovely childbed after such travail!
The cook – dear me, how cruel are our kitchen queens!
Humanity won't mix with cabbages and beans!
She wanted me to drown five kittens out of six,
Five helpless Mayday kits, of all the cruel tricks
To murder five white kittens (with black tails)! But I,
I gave her such a wigging, said they *must* not die!
Thank goodness I was merciful, my six survived;
It was not long before they all grew up and thrived.
Below the window of my angry cook at night
They all lift up their voices, singing with delight.
A year has gone and Mayday's here again once more;
Six Maycats and their Mum have beds on every floor
And all the seven cats have seven kittens each,
Maykittens, white, black tails, depriving Cook of speech.

She rages like a Fury, but I firmly will decline
To do as Fury wants and drown all forty-nine!
To be humane so often leaves you in a fix;
Last May I had one cat and now I've fifty-six!

after *Von Katzen*, by Theodor Woldsen Storm

Tybert and Reynart

The complaynt of the bere upon the foxe

I complayne to yow mercyful lorde syre kynge so as ye may see how that
I am handled prayeng you t(o)auenge it vpon reynart the felle beest ffor
I haue goten this in your seruyse. I haue loste bothe my formest feet my
chekes and myn eeris by his false deceyte and treson.

The kynge sayde how durst this fals theef Reynart doo this I saye
to yow bruyn and swere by my crowne I shal so auenge you on hym that
ye shal conne me thanke

he sente for alle the wyse beestis and desired counseyl how that he
myght auenge this ouer grete wronge that the foxe had don Thenne the
counseyl concluded olde and yong that he shold be sente fore and dayed
ernestly again for t(o) abyde suche Iugement as shold there be gyuen on
hym of alle his trespaces And they thought that the catte tybert myght
best do this message yf he wolde for he is right wyse The kynge thought
this counceyl good

How the kynge sente another tyme tybert the catte
for the foxe, and how tybert spedde with reynart the foxe

Thenne the kynge saide sir tybert ye shal now goo to reynart and saye to
hym this seconde tyme that he come to court vnto the plee for to answere
for though he be felle to other beestis he trusteth you wel and shal doo
by your counseyl and telle yf he come not he shal haue the thirde warnyng
and be dayed and yf he thenne come not we shal procede by ryght
ayenste hym and alle hys lygnage wythout mercy

Tybert spack My lord the kynge they that this counseylde you were not
my frendes what shal I doo there he wil not for me neyther come ne
abyde I beseche you dere Kynge sende some other to hym I am lytyl and
feble bruyn the bere whiche was so grete and stronge coude not brynge
hym how shold I thenne take it on honde

Nay said the kynge sir tybert ye ben wyse and wel lerned Though ye
be not grete ther lyeth not on many do more wyth crafte and connyng
than with myght and strengthe

Thenne said the catte syth it muste nedes be don I muste thenne take it
upon me god yeue grace that I may wel achieue it for my herte is heuy
and euil willed therto

Tybert made hym sone redy toward maleperduys and he saw fro ferre come fleyng one of seynt martyns byrdes tho cryde he lowde and saide al hayl gentyl byrde torne thy wynges hetherward and flee on my right side the byrde flewh forth vpon a tree whiche stoode on the lift side of the catte tho was tybert woo ffor he thought hit was a shrewd token and a sygne of harme for yf the birde had flowen on his right side he had ben mery and glad but now he sorowed that his Iourney shold torne to unhappe neuertheles he dyde as many doo and gaf to hym self better hope than his herte sayde he wente and ronne to maleperduys ward and there he fonde the foxe allone standynge to fore his hous

Tybert saide The riche god yeue you good euen reynart the kyng hath menaced yow for to take your lyf from yow yf ye come not now wyth me to the court

The foxe tho spack and said Tibert my dere cosyn ye be right wel come I wolde wel truly that ye had moche good lucke what hurted the foxe to speke fayre though he sayd wel his herte thoughte it not and that shal be seen er they departe

reynart sayde wylle we this nyght be to gydre I wyl make you good chyere and to morow erly in the dawnyng we wyl to gydre goo to the court good neue late us so doo I haue none of my kyn that I truste so moche to as to yow hier was bruyn the bere the traytour he loked so shrewdly on me and me thoughte he was so stronge that I wolde not for a thousand marke haue goon with hym but cosyn I wil to morow erly goo with yow

Tybert saide it is beste that we now goo for the mone shyneth also light as it were daye I neuer sawe fayrer weder nay dere cosyn suche might mete vs by daye tyme that wold make vs good chiere and by nyghtte parauenture myght doo vs harme it is suspecyous to walke by nyghte. Therfore abyde this nyght here by me

Tybert sayde what sholde we ete yf we abode here

reynart sayde here is but lytel to ete ye maye wel haue an hony combe good and swete what saye ye Tybert wyl ye ony therof.

tybert answerd I sette nought therby haue ye nothyng ellis yf ye gaf me agood fatte mows I shold be better plesyd

a fatte mows said reynard dere cosyn what saye ye here by dwelleth a preest and hath a barne by his hows ther in ben so many myse that a man shold not lede them a way vpon a wayne I haue herd the preest many tymes complayne that they dyde hym moche harme

O dere reyner lede me thyder for alle that I may doo for yow yea tybert saye ye me trouthe loue ye wel myes

yf I loue hem wel said the catte I loue myes better than ony thyng that men gyue me. knowe ye not that myes sauoure better than veneson ye than flawnes or pasteyes wil ye wel doo. so lede me theder where the myes ben. and thenne shal ye wynne my loue. yea al had ye slayn my fader moder and alle my kyn.

Reynart sayd ye moke and Jape therwyth.

the catte saide so helpe me god I doo not.

Tybert said the foxe wiste I that veryly I wolde yet this nyght make that ye shuld be ful of myes.

reynart quod he ful that were many.

tyberte ye Iape

reynart quod he in trouth I doo not yf I hadde a fatte mows I wold not gyue it for a golden noble

late vs goo thenne tybert quod the foxe I wyl brynge yow to the place er I goo fro you

reyner quod the foxe (*or rather* the cat) vpon your saufconduyt I wolde wel goo wyth you to monpelier

late vs thenne goo said the foxe we tarye alto longe

Thus wente they forth withoute lettyng to the place where as they wold be to the prestes barne whiche was faste wallid aboute with a mude wal and the nyght to fore the foxe had broken in and had stolen fro the preest a good fatte henne and the preest alle angry had sette a gryn to fore the hool to auenge hym for he wold fayn haue take the foxe this knewe wel the felle theef the foxe And said sir tybert cosyn crepe into this hool and ye shal not longe tarye but that ye shal catche myes by grete heepis herke how they pype. whan ye be ful come agayn I wil tarye here after you be fore this hole we wil to morowe goo to gyder to the court. Tybert why tarye ye thus longe come off and so maye we retorne sone to my wyf. whiche wayteth after vs and shal make vs good chiere

Tybert saide reynart cosyn is it thenne your counseyl that I goo in to this hole. Thise prestes ben so wyly and shrewyssh I drede to take harme

O ho tybert said the foxe I sawe you neuer so sore aferde what eyleth yow

the catte was ashamed and sprange in to the hoole. And anon he was caught in the gryn by the necke er he wyste thus deceyuyd reynart his ghest and cosyn

As tybert was waer of the grynne he was a ferde and sprange forth the grynne wente to thenne he began he to wrawen for he was almost y stranglyd he called he cryed and made a shrewd noyse

reynart stode to fore the hool and herde al and was wel a payed and sayde tybert loue ye wel myes be they fatte and good knewe the preeste herof or mertynet they be so gentyl that they wolde brynge yow sawce Tybert ye synge and eten is that the guyse of the court lord god yf ysegrym ware there by yow in suche reste as ye now be thenne shold I be glad for ofte he hath don me scathe and harme

tybert coude not goo awaye but he mawede and galped so lowde that martynet sprang vp and cryde lowde god be thanked my gryn hath taken the theef that hath stolen our hennes aryse vp we wil rewarde hym

Wyth these wordes aroose the preest in an euyl tyme and waked alle them that were in the hows and cryde wyth a lowede vois the foxe is take

there leept and ranne alle that there was. the preest hym self ranne al
moder naked mertynet was the first that cam to tybert the preest toke to
locken his wyf an offryng candel and bad her lyght it atte fyer and he
smote tybert with a grete staf Ther receyuid tybert many a grete stroke
ouer alle his body mertynet was so angry that he smote the catte an eye
out the naked preest lyfte vp and shold haue gyuen a grete stroke to
tybert but tybert that sawe that he muste deye sprange bytwene the
prestes legges wyth his clawes and with his teeth that he raught out his
ryght colyon or balock stone that leep becam yl to the preest and to his
grete shame.

This thynge fyl doun vpon the floer whan dame Iulocke knewe that
she sware by her faders sowle that she wolde it had coste her alle the
offryng of a hole yere that the preest had not had that harme hurte and
shame and that it had not happed and said in the deueles name was the
grynne there sette see mertynet lyef sone this is of thy faders harneys
This is a grete shame and to me a grete hurte for though he be heled
herof yet he is but a loste man to me and also shal neuer conne doo that
swete playe and game

The foxe stode wythoute to fore the hole and herde alle thyse wordes
and lawhed so sore that he vnnethe coude stonde he spack thus al softly
dame Iulock be al stylle and your grete sorowe synke Al hath the preest
loste one of his stones it shal not hyndre hym he shal doo wyth you wel
ynowh ther is in the world many a chapel in whiche is rongen but one belle
thus scorned and mocked the foxe the prestes wyf dam iulock that was ful
of sorowe

The preest fyl doun a swoune they toke hym vp and brought hym
agayn to bedde. tho wente the foxe agayn in to his borugh ward and lefte
tybert the catte in grete drede and Ieopardye for the foxe wiste none
other but that the catte was nygh deed but whan tybert the catte sawe
them al besy aboute the preest tho began he to byte and gnawe the
grenne in the myddel a sondre and sprange out of the hool and wente
rollyng and wentlyng towards the kyng's court or he cam theder it was
fayr day and the sonne began to ryse And he cam to the court as a poure
wyght he had caught harme atte prestes hows by the helpe and counseyl
of the foxe his body was al to beten and blynde on the one eye whan the
kynge wyste this that tybert was thus arayed he was sore angry and
menaced reynart the theef sore and anone gadred his counseyl to wyte
what they wold aduyse hym how he myght brynge the foxe to the lawe
and how he sholde be fette

from the popular mediaeval romance,
translated and printed by William Caxton in 1481

Belling the cat

The fable of the mice planning to bell the cat was a favourite in the Middle Ages. La Fontaine has it in his *Fables* but it does not appear to have been of ancient origin. It is told inimitably in *The vision concerning Piers Plowman*, attributed to William Langland, who is said to have written the poem between 1360 and 1399. (It also appears in a collection of fables written by Marie de France, a French poetess of the late twelfth century who lived in England. Her collection was called *Ysopet*.)

With that ran ther a route
Of ratons at ones,
And smale mees myd hem
Mo than a thousand,
And comen to a counseil
For the commune profit;
For a cat of a contree
Cam whan hym liked,
And overleep hem lightliche,
And laughte hem at his wille,
And pleide with hem perillousli,
And possed aboute.
'For doute of diverse dredes,
We dar noght wel loke;
And if we grucche of his gamen,
He wol greven us alle,
Cracchen us or clawen us,
And in hise clouches holde,
That us lotheth the lif
Er he late us passe.
Mighte we with any wit
His wille withstonde,
We mighte be lordes o-lofte,
And lyven at our ese.'
A raton of renoun,
Moost renable of tongue,
Seide for a sovereyn
Help to hymselve:
'I have y-seyen segges,' quod he
'In the cité of Londone,

Beren beighes ful brighte
Abouten hire nekkes,
And somme colers of crafty werk;
Uncoupled thei wenten
Bothe in wareyne and in waast
Where hemself liked.
And outher while thei arn elliswhere,
As I here telle;
Were ther a belle on hire beighe,
By Jhesu, as me thynketh,
Men myghte witen wher thei wente,
And awey renne!'
    'And right so,' quod that raton,
'Reson me sheweth,
To bugge a belle of bras,
Or of bright silver,
And knytten it on a coler
For oure commune profit,
Wher he ryt or rest,
Or renneth to pleye;
And if hym list for to laike,
Thanne loke we mowen,
And peeren in his presence
The while him pleye liketh:
And, if hym wratheth, be war,
And his way shonye.'
   Al this route of ratons
To this reson thei assented.
Ac tho the belle was y-brought,
And on the beighe hanged,
Ther ne was raton in al the route,
For al the reaume of Fraunce,
That dorste have bounden the belle
About the cattes nekke,
Ne hangen it aboute the cattes hals,
Al Engelond to wynne.
Alle helden hem un-hardy,
And hir counseil feble;
And leten hire labour lost
And al hire longe studie.
   A mous that muche good
Kouthe, as me thoughte,
Strook forth sternely,
And stood bifore hem alle,
And to the route of ratons

Reherced thise wordes:
    'Though we killen the cat,
Yet sholde ther come another
To cacchen us and al oure kynde,
Though we cropen under benches.
For-thi I counseille al the commune
To late the cat worthe;
And be we nevere bolde
The belle hym to shewe;
For I herde my sire seyn,
Is seven yeer y-passed,
Ther the cat is a kitone
The court is ful elenge;
That witnesseth holy writ,
Who so wole it rede:
Vae terrae ubi puer rex est! etc.
For may no renk ther reste have
For ratons by nyghte;
The while he caccheth conynges,
He coveiteth noght youre caroyne,
But fedeth hym al with venyson:
Defame we hym nevere.
For better is a litel los
Than a long sorwe,
The maze among us alle,
Theigh we mysse a sherewe;
For many mennes malt
We mees wolde destruye,
And also ye route of ratons
Rende mennes clothes,
Nere the cat of that court
That can yow over-lepe;
For hadde ye rattes youre wille,
Ye kouthe noght rule yow selve.'
    'I seye for me,' quod the mous,
'I se so muchel after,
Shal nevere the cat ne the kiton
By my counseil be greved,
Thorugh carpynge of this coler
That costed me nevere
And though it hadde costned me catel,
Bi-knowen it I nolde,
But suffren, as hymself wolde,
To doon as hym liketh,
Coupled and uncoupled

To cacche what thei mowe.
For-thi ech a wis wight I warne,
Wite wel his owene.'
   What this metels by-meneth,
Ye men that ben murye
Devyne ye, for I ne dar,
By deere God in hevene.

Glossary

raton *rat*
mees *mice*
myd *with*
hem *them*
laughte *caught*
pleide *played*
possed *pushed*
grucche *grudge*
greven *trouble*
cracchen *scratch*
clawen *stroke*
renable *reasonable*
seide *said*
y-seyen *seen*
segges *men*
beren *wearing*
beighes *necklets*
uncoupled *alone*
wareyne *warren*
waast *wilderness*
outher while *at other times*
hire *their*
witen *know*
bugge *buy*
knytten *fasten*
ryt *rode*
laike *play*
loke *watch*

mowen *could*
peeren *appear*
shonye *shun*
ac tho *but when*
hals *throat*
un-hardy *cowardly*
kouthe *knew*
strook *struck*
cacchen *catch*
cropen *crept*
for-thi *therefore*
late the cat worthe *let the cat be*
ther the cat is a kitone *when the cat is kitten*
elenge *sorrowful, wretched*
renk *man*
ther *then*
conynges *rabbits*
caroyne *flesh*
theigh *though*
carpynge *chatter*
catel *treasure*
bi-knowen *acknowledge*
nolde *would not*
for-thi ech . . . ownes *wherefore I warn each wise creature to guard well his own*
metels *dream*
murye *merry*

To Mrs Reynolds' cat

Cat! who hast pass'd thy grand climacteric,
  How many mice and rats hast in thy days
  Destroy'd? – How many tit bits stolen? Gaze
With those bright languid segments green, and prick
Those velvet ears – but pr'ythee do not stick
  Thy latent talons in me – and upraise
  Thy gentle mew – and tell me all thy frays
Of fish and mice, and rats and tender chick.
Nay, look not down, nor lick thy dainty wrists –
  For all the wheezy asthma, – and for all
Thy tail's tip is nick'd off – and though the fists
  Of many a maid have given thee many a maul,
Still is that fur as soft as when the lists
  In youth thou enter'dst on glass bottled wall.

John Keats

Mourka

The hero-cat of Stalingrad

To the historic company which is headed by Puss-in-Boots, to which belong the cat in the adage, Dick Whittington's Cat and those of Cheshire and Kilkenny, there has been added a new member well deserving the honour. This is Mourka, the Cat of Stalingrad. He used, so we are told, to carry messages as to enemy gun emplacements from a group of Russian scouts to a house across the street. The words 'used to' are ominous, for death stalks abroad in the streets of Stalingrad. We know not whether his nine lives sufficed to see Mourka safe across or whether (the mind is strangely haunted by proverbs) the care of his high office killed him. He may, like Felix, keep on walking that deadly path or, as it is pleasanter to think, he may live retired with plenty of milk after his long and gallant service. All we do know is that if he has a mind to look at a king no one dare deny him that privilege. As Dr Johnson said of Hodge, he is a very fine cat, a very fine cat indeed.

In deeds of heroism dogs have hitherto occupied a far more conspicuous place than cats, and Mourka has done much to redress the balance. To this particular service indeed the cat is by far the better adapted. His stealthy air may suggest the stage spy who is easily detected, but in real life no one would suspect him save a bird or a mouse. He bears himself so independently that it is impossible to believe that he would condescend to run on messages. If in a good cause he did so demean himself, he would never betray his errand. A dog in similar circumstances is too consciously pleased with himself. If he brings back a newspaper from the shop or takes letters to the post, he carries his head high, as one who should say 'See how vast a trust my master reposes in me'. Not so the cat.

'Dumb, inscrutable and grand' he is palpably concerned with his own private affairs which are nothing to anybody.

There are always persons ready to expose the petty weaknesses of the great and to attribute to them motives lower than the heroic. So it may be even with Mourka. It appears that the company kitchen was situated in the house to which he bore dispatches, and some, with the cavilling peculiar to vulgar minds, will see in this more than a coincidence. That he was warmly greeted in the kitchen after his perilous journey we may rest assured. That he took an innocent pleasure in looking forward to the welcome of his comrades we may perhaps imagine. Beyond that the name of Mourka must never be coupled with a breath of doubt. He has shown himself worthy of Stalingrad, and whether for cat or man there can be no higher praise.

Fourth Leader, *The Times*, 13 January 1943

Keeper of the gate, British Museum 1909–29

There once lived in Bloomsbury a cat named Black Jack, who, like many other denizens of the district, found the Reading Room of the British Museum an irresistible attraction. He used to sit, looking like one of his remote Egyptian ancestors, upright upon the reading-desks. Readers always treated Black Jack with consideration and would open the door for him when he wanted to go out.

On one occasion Black Jack failed to find a door-opener and was imprisoned in a room where the bound volumes of newspapers were kept. When later released he was discovered to have occupied his time in sharpening his claws on the bindings. It was decreed that Black Jack MUST GO.

However, despite the decree of ostracism, Black Jack found secret asylum with certain sympathetic officials. He was reported 'Missing presumed dead', but after a time he emerged from his asylum and to everyone's satisfaction resumed his duties as Reading Room Cat.

One day Black Jack, who, as a result of his adventure, must have been ruminating on how to find a successor, brought a kitten to the Museum and presented it, with a just appreciation of the proprieties, to the Keeper of the Egyptian Mummied Cats. The kitten was accepted by the cats who already lived in the Keeper's official house. He became 'Mike' and as such grew to be even more famous than his sponsor, Black Jack. Though perhaps not a sociable cat, he became a close friend of the Gate-keeper, eventually deciding to make the lodge his principal residence. There he would sit upon a ledge, checking members of the public as they went in and out.

When the colonnade was peopled only by pigeons on Sunday mornings, one of the house cats taught Mike how to stalk them. Mesmerized by the two cats, the pigeons would become silly and fall over, whereupon the cats would each seize a bird and take it into the house, where they were given milk and meat as a reward. It is recorded that the pigeons generally recovered and flew off to rejoin their companions.

Mike was the subject of an obituary by Sir Ernest Wallis Budge and poems in his memory were written by F. C. W. Hiley, an Assistant Keeper of Printed Books and by Dr Arundell Esdaile, Secretary of the Museum at the time. Many more famous characters have had less distinguished biographers. Dr Esdaile's lines suggest that he felt that Mike was a somewhat cross-grained character – that failure, when young, to catch pigeons had soured him despite later success. Then follow the astonishing lines:

Then swelled the cynic rage which these began
At the approach of unofficial man.

What cat *could* suffer from 'cynic' rage?

There is in existence a picture of Mike, which shows a rather cross though obviously learned tabby; and no doubt Mike acquired in his long official life the Civil Servant's attitude to his masters. At any rate, the verse ends:

I scorned the public as it came and went,
To blandishments and fish indifferent,
But sat for nineteen years and Kept the Gate,
In every hair an Officer of State.

The Great Cat Ra

I am the Cat which fought hard by the Persea Tree in Annu (Heliopolis) on the night when the foes of Neb-er-tcher were destroyed.

Who is this Cat?

This male Cat is Ra himself and he was called Mau because of the speech of the god Sa, who said concerning him:

'He is like unto that which he hath made, therefore did the name of Ra become Mau.' Others, however, say that the male cat is the god Shu, who made over the possessions of Keb to Osiris.

from the Papyrus of Nebseni, in the British Museum,
tr. by Sir Ernest Budge, in the *Book of the Dead*

The Papyrus of Ani and the Papyrus of Hunefer, both in the British Museum, have each a painting showing a great cat holding a knife in its forepaw, with which it is cutting off the head of a monstrous python. The Cat is Ra and the python is the symbol of Set, the arch-enemy of Ra. . . . The slaying of the python by the Cat is symbolic of the famous slaughter of the foes of Ra, or Osiris. . . .

note by Sir Ernest Budge

In praise of Ra

Praise be to thee, O Ra, exalted Sekhem, thou art the Great Cat, the avenger of the gods, and the judge of words, and the president of the sovereign chiefs and the governor of the holy Circle; thou art indeed the bodies of the Great Cat.

from the Seventy-five Praises of Ra, inscribed on the walls
of royal tombs of the XIXth and XXth Dynasties of Thebes

The cats and the viper

Passing from the green-house into the barn I saw three kittens (we have so many in our retinue) looking with fixed attention at something which lay on the threshold of a door curled up. I took but little notice of them at first but a loud hiss engaged me to attend more closely, when behold, a viper! The largest I remember to have seen, rearing itself, darting its forked tongue and ejaculating the aforementioned hiss at the nose of a kitten almost in contact with his lips. I ran into the hall for a hoe with a long handle, with which I intended to assail him, and returning in a few seconds missed him: he was gone and I feared had escaped me. Still however the kitten sat watching immovably in the same spot. I concluded therefore that, sliding between the door and the threshold, he had found his way out of the garden into the yard. I went round immediately and there found him in close conversation with the old cat, whose curiosity being excited by so novel an experience, inclined her to pat his head repeatedly with her fore-foot; with her claws, however, sheathed, and not in anger, but in the way of philosophical enquiry and examination.

To prevent her falling a victim to so laudable an exercise of her talents, I interposed in a moment with the hoe and performed upon him an act of decapitation which, though not immediately mortal, proved so in the end. Had he slid into the passages, where it is dark, or had he, when in the yard, met no interruption from the cat and secreted himself in one of the out-houses, it is hardly possible but that some of the family must have been bitten.

letter from William Cowper to the Rev. William Unwin, 3 August 1782

Cats' eyes

The cat clock

One day, when we went to pay a visit to some families of Chinese Christian peasants, we met, near a farm, a young lad, who was taking a buffalo to graze along our path. We asked him carelessly, as we passed, whether it was yet noon. The child raised his head to look at the sun, but it was hidden behind thick clouds, and he could read no answer there. 'The sky is so cloudy,' said he, 'but wait a moment;' and with these words he ran towards the farm, and came back a few minutes afterwards with a cat in his arms. 'Look here,' said he; 'It is not noon yet;' and he showed us the cat's eyes, by pushing up the lids with his hands. We looked at the child with surprise, but he was evidently in earnest: and the cat, though astonished, and not much pleased with the experiment made on her eyes, behaved with most exemplary complaisance. 'Very well,' said we, 'thank you;' and he then let go the cat, who made her escape pretty quickly, and we continued our route. . . .

As soon as ever we reached the farm, however, we made haste to ask our Christians whether they could tell the clock by looking into a cat's eyes. . . . They brought us three or four, and explained in what manner they might be made use of for watches. They pointed out that the pupil of their eyes went on constantly growing narrower until twelve o'clock, when they became like a fine line, as thin as a hair, drawn perpendicularly across the eye, and that after twelve the dilatation recommenced.

from Mrs J. Sinnett's translation *The Chinese Empire*
from the French of Père Évariste Régis Huc, French Missionary and traveller, 1854

A 'lunatic' beast

Just as the lion is a creature that belongs to the sun, so is the cat a lunatic beast – (that is, a beast governed by the moon). Its eyes see clearly and gleam in the darkest nights. They wax and wane in conformity with the phases of the moon. Just as the moon has some of the properties of the light of the sun and so offers a new face every day, so the cat is influenced by a similar relationship with the moon. The pupil of a cat's eye dilates and contracts in conjunction with the heavenly body, being crescent or on the wane in sympathy. Some naturalists maintain that when the moon is full, cats have more power and skill in their warring against mice than when there is no moon.

from *La Science Héroïque*
by Vulsan de la Colombière

The cat and the moon

The cat went here and there
And the moon spun round like a top,
And the nearest kin of the moon,
The creeping cat, looked up.
Black Minnaloushe stared at the moon,
For, wander and wail as he would,
The pure cold light in the sky
Troubled his animal blood.
Minnaloushe runs in the grass
Lifting his delicate feet.
Do you dance, Minnaloushe, do you dance?
When two close kindred meet,
What better than call a dance?
Maybe the moon may learn,
Tired of that courtly fashion,
A new dance turn.
Minnaloushe creeps through the grass
From moonlit place to place,
The sacred moon overhead
Has taken a new phase.
Does Minnaloushe know that his pupils
Will pass from change to change,
And that from round to crescent
From crescent to round they range?
Minnaloushe creeps through the grass
Alone, important and wise,
And lifts to the changing moon
His changing eyes.

William Butler Yeats

To my cat, Coquette

Switch on your eyes, Coquette!
It's just too dark to see –
A poet's lamp, my pet!

By gloom I'll be beset,
White wanton, if you flee.
Switch on your eyes, Coquette!

No candle's ready yet;
Sole hope you are for me –
A poet's lamp, my pet!

There's Jane with my Gazette!
A note upon my knee!
Switch on your eyes, Coquette!

Old friends have birthdays yet!
Ah, one's inviting me!
A poet's lamp, my pet!

When dressing, some may fret
Without a glass to see.
Switch on your eyes, Coquette!
A poet's lamp, my pet!

after the villanelle by the French poet Joseph Boulmier

Parson Woodforde's stiony

(Stiony, more usually Styany, is a contraction of 'Sty-on-eye')

The Stiony on my right Eye-lid still swelled and inflamed very much. As
it is commonly said that the Eye-lid being rubbed by the tail of a black
Cat would do it much good if not entirely cure it, and having a black Cat,
a little before dinner I made a trial of it, and very soon after dinner I
found my Eye-lid much abated of the swelling and almost free from Pain.
I cannot therefore but conclude it to be of the greatest service to a Stiony
on the Eye-lid. Any other Cat's Tail may have the above effect in all
probability – but I did my Eye-lid with my own black Tom Cat's Tail.

The Rev. James Woodforde, 11 March 1791

To a cat

Stately, kindly, lordly friend,
   Condescend
Here to sit by me, and turn
Glorious eyes that smile and burn,
Golden eyes, love's lustrous meed,
On the golden page I read.

All your wondrous wealth of hair,
   Dark and fair,
Silken-shaggy, soft and bright
As the clouds and beams of night,
Pays my reverent hand's caress
Back with friendlier gentleness.

Dogs may fawn on all and some
   As they come;
You, a friend of loftier mind,
Answer friends alone in kind.
Just your foot upon my hand
Softly bids it understand.

A. C. Swinburne

Madame Théophile

Madame Théophile, a reddish cat with a white breast, a pink nose and blue eyes, was so called because she lived with me in an intimacy that was quite conjugal, sleeping at the foot of my bed, dreaming on the arm of my chair while I wrote, going down to the garden and following me in my walks, assisting at my meals, and sometimes even intercepting a tit-bit on its way from the plate to my mouth.

One day a friend of mine who was going away for a few days brought me his parrot to look after during his absence. The bird, feeling himself to be among strangers, had climbed to the top of his perch by the help of his beak, and was rolling his eyes, which were like brass-headed nails, and blinking the white skin which served him for eyelids, in a decidedly frightened way.

Madame Théophile had never seen a parrot, and this new creature evidently caused her much surprise. Motionless as an embalmed Egyptian cat in its wrappings, she watched the bird with an air of profound meditation, putting together all the notions of natural history which she had been able to gather on the roof, in the yard, or in the garden. The shadow of her thoughts passed across her opalescent eyes, and I could read in them this summary of her investigations:

'That is certainly a green chicken.'

Having arrived at this conclusion, the cat jumped down from the table on which she had established her post of observation, and retired to a corner of the room, where she flattened herself on the floor with elbows out and head down, all ready to spring, like the blank panther in Gérome's picture, watching the gazelles drinking at the lake.

The parrot followed the cat's movements with feverish anxiety. His feathers bristled, he rattled his chain, raised one foot and agitated his toes and whetted his beak on the edge of the food-box. His instinct told him that this was an enemy meditating some evil deed. As to the cat's eyes, which were fixed on the bird with fascinating intensity, they said in language which the parrot understood perfectly, for there was nothing ambiguous about it, 'Although it is green, this chicken must be good to eat.'

I followed the scene with interest, ready to intervene if necessity arose. Madame Théophile had insensibly drawn nearer. Her pink nose quivered, she half closed her eyes, and her contractile claws went in and out. Little shivers ran down her spine, as they do down a gourmet's who is just going to sit down to a fat truffled pullet. She gloated over the idea of the rare and succulent feast she was going to enjoy. This exotic dish excited all her greediness. Suddenly her back was bent like a bow, and in one vigorous, elastic bound she alighted on the perch. The parrot, perceiving the danger, promptly exclaimed in a bass voice, as solemn and deep as that of Monsieur Joseph Prudhomme: 'As tu déjeuné, Jacquot?' This speech caused the cat to spring back in unspeakable terror. A blare of trumpets, a crash of broken crockery, or a pistol fired close to her ear would not have produced wilder alarm. All her ornithological ideas were upset.

The parrot continued:

'Et de quoi? De roti du roi.'

The cat's face clearly expressed: 'This is not a bird; it is a gentleman; he is speaking!'

'Quand j'ai bu du vin clairet
Tout tourne, tout tourne au cabaret'

sang the parrot in a deafening voice, for he had grasped the fact that the alarm caused by his speech was his best defence.

The cat cast a look full of interrogation at me, and not being satisfied with my reply she went and hid herself under the bed, where she remained the rest of the day.

People who are not in the habit of living with animals, and who, like Descartes, see nothing more in them than mere machines, will no doubt think that I am attributing ideas to the bird and the beast which were never theirs, but I have done no more than translate them into human language. The next day Madame Théophile, feeling somewhat re-assured, attempted another attack, which was repulsed in the same way. After that she resigned herself to the inevitable, and accepted the bird as a man.

This dainty and charming animal loved perfumes, some kinds of which threw her into ecstasies.

She also had a taste for music. Seated on a pile of scores, she would listen attentively and with evident pleasure to the ladies who came to my house to sing. But shrill notes made her nervous, and when the high A occurred she always shut the singer's mouth with her paw.

We often amused ourselves by trying this experiment with her, and never found it fail. This dilettante of a cat never mistook the note.

from *La Ménagerie Intime* by Théophile Gautier (1811–72)
tr. by Lady Chance

Note: Strangely, there is a much more ancient story of a cat and parrot. The date is round about A.D. 650. The cruel Empress Wu Chao of China had a cat and a parrot who were trained to eat out of the same dish. One day the Empress decided that this friendliness should be exhibited to all the court. Unhappily before the exhibition was over, the cat, whose hunger was unappeased, seized the parrot and ate it, much to the Empress's embarrassment.

Five eyes

In Hans' old mill his three black cats
Watch the bins for the thieving rats.
Whisker and claw, they crouch in the night,
Their five eyes smouldering green and bright:
Squeaks from the flour sacks, squeaks from where
The cold wind stirs on the empty stair,
Squeaking and scampering everywhere.
Then down they pounce, now in, now out,
At whisking tail, and sniffing snout;
While lean old Hans, he snores away
Till peep of light and break of day;
Then up he climbs to his creaking mill,
Out come his cats all grey with meal,
Jekkel, and Jessop and one-eyed Jill.

Walter de la Mare

Mina and Clementina

A beautiful peasant girl of the village of Monteorsano in the Brianza, had obtained a sort of melancholy celebrity by an infliction which frequently struck her down to the earth, in the midst of the village festival, or church ceremony, where her beauty and piety were the boast and edification of her village friends. Every physician in Lombardy, every saint in the calendar, had been applied to on behalf of Clementina; and vows and offerings had been made in vain to cure what was incurable, a confirmed epilepsy. If the saints, however, were negligent, Clementina had one friend whose vigilance never slumbered. It was her cat, which not only shared her bed and her polenta but followed her in her walks and devotions, from the vineyards to the altar.

The first time that Mina saw her young mistress fall in a fit and wound herself against a tomb in the village cemetery, she exhibited the most extraordinary emotion. She soon acquired the habit, from the frequent recurrence of the infirmity, of watching its approach; and at last seemed to have obtained such a knowledge of the change of countenance and colour which preceded the attack, that she was wont on the first symptom to run to the parents of Clementina, and by dragging their clothes, scratching at their persons or mewing in the most melancholy manner she succeeded in awakening their attention and trotted out before them, mewing them on to the spot where her young mistress lay lifeless. Mina at last obtained such confidence for her warnings that on the first cry of the faithful cat, the friends of Clementina flew to her assistance before she incurred any injury from her sudden fall.

At fifteen the malady of the beautiful Clementina brought her to the tomb. Her cat walked after the bier, on which she was exposed as is the custom in Italy, and covered with flowers. During the funeral service she sat at the head of the bier, gazing with an intent look on the lifeless features of her young mistress; and when the grave was filling she made a vain endeavour to jump in, but was withheld by the bystanders who carried home this chief mourner after the melancholy ceremony.

Mina, however, was seen the next morning stretched upon the new-made grave, which she continued to visit daily until she visited it for the last time; a few months after her friend's death she was found dead upon the green mound that covered her remains.

The celebrity of the 'Gatto del Cimitero' has not yet passed away from the village of Monteorsano.

from *The Book of the Boudoir* by Lady Morgan

Some Chinese cats

Ch'en Hai-sang's cat

The family of Mr Ch'en Hai-sang in the Eastern part of the city wall of T'ai-ho Hsien had a cat and she always followed him about. A few years after, he died; she would not eat from morning to night and lay down by his coffin. She died after seven days .

from the *Chi-an Fu Chin* ed. by Wang Shih-huai, sixteenth century

Tiger Cat

The family of Ch'i Yen kept a cat, and he considered it wonderful, telling people that its name was 'Tiger Cat' . A stranger said to him, 'A tiger is certainly fierce but not so mysterious as a dragon. I request you to change its name into "Dragon Cat".' Another stranger said to him, 'A dragon is certainly more mysterious than a tiger; when it ascends to the sky, it requires the floating clouds. Thus the clouds are superior to a dragon. Why not call it "Cloud Cat"?' Then another one said to him, 'When the clouds conceal the sky, the wind will suddenly disperse them. The clouds are no match for the wind. Please change its name into "Wind Cat".' Yet another one said to him, 'When a gale rises violently, we screen from it with walls which are good enough for protection. What can the wind do to the walls? It is appropriate to call it "Wall Cat".'

Yet another one said to him, 'The walls are certainly strong, but when the rats make holes through them, they will collapse. What can the wall do to the rats? It is correct to call it "Rat Cat".'

An old man of Tung-li laughed at all of them and remarked, 'Alas! Alas! A cat is a cat. It is to catch rats. Why do they make it lose its real nature?'

from the *Hsien-i* by Liu Yuan-ch'ing

Dragon with two horns

In the middle of the Chia-ching period (A.D. 1522–1566) there was a cat
in the palace. She was of faintly blue colour but her two eyebrows were
clearly jade-white and she was called Shuang-mei (Frost-Eyebrows). She
surmised the Emperor's intentions very well. Whomever His Majesty
summoned and wherever her Imperial Master went, she always led. She
waited upon the Emperor until he slept and then she lay still like a stump.

His Majesty was very fond of her, and when she died, ordered that she
should be buried in the north side of the Wan-sui mountains (in Peking,
now Peping). By her grave was erected a stone tablet inscribed with three
characters: 'Ch'iu-lung Chung' (Grave of a Dragon with two horns).
(An allegorical term for a superior man.)

from the *Erh-t'an* by Wang T'ung-kuei

Chang T'uan's seven cats

The first was called 'Tung-shou' (Eastern Guard).
The second was called 'Pai-feng' (White Phoenix).
The third was called 'Tzu-ying' (Purple Flower).
The fourth was called 'Ch'u-fen' (Expelling Vexation).
The fifth was called 'Chin-tai' (Brocade Belt).
The sixth was called 'Yun-t'u' (Picture of Clouds).
The seventh was called 'Wan-kuan' (A myriad of strings of 1000 each).
Every one of them was worth several pieces of gold.

in the *Chi-shih Chu,* attributed to Feng Chih,
but probably written by Wang Chih, *circa* 1100

The story of Minette

In 1844, Pierre-Jules Hetzel, whose pen-name was P.-J. Stahl, published in Paris a collection of stories, or fantasies, called *Scènes de la Vie Privée et Publique des Animaux*. The book, which contained many brilliant and witty drawings by Grandville, had contributions from a number of well-known authors, including Honoré de Balzac and George Sand. One of these, which has not hitherto appeared in English, is the story of a cat named Beauty, otherwise Minette, entitled *Peines de Coeur d'une Chatte Anglaise*, by Balzac, and is a satire on the hypocrisy of English society.

In it, Beauty, married to an aristocratic but stuffy English cat, has a dashing affair with a young French cat named Brisquet, an attaché at the French Embassy. Alas, a nephew of Beauty's husband finds it out; there is a divorce and the tale ends with Brisquet's murder.

There is, however, a sequel written by Stahl in the form of letters between Beauty, or Minette, and her sister Bébé, in which Minette explains that the *Peines de Coeur* was a wicked libel by Brisquet himself; Minette's own version of what happened to her is told in the extracts from her letters which follow Balzac's story (*below*).

The love affairs of an English cat

I was born in the house of a clergyman in Catshire, near the little town of Miaulbury. The fertility of my mother condemned nearly all her children to a cruel fate, for you know that no one has been able to assign a cause for the maternal intemperance of English cats, which threatens to populate the entire world. Both toms and tabbies in turn attribute this result to their amiability and to their own special virtues. But some irreverent observers say that toms and tabbies in England are subject to such utterly boring rules, that they find their only amusements in these little family diversions. Others believe that matters of business and high policy are involved, because of English rule in India; but such considerations are hardly appropriate for my paws, and I leave them to the *Edinburgh Review*.

I was saved from the statutory drowning because of my pure white coat. And they called me 'Beauty'. But alas, the poverty of the clergyman, who had a wife and eleven daughters, prevented him from keeping me. An elderly spinster noticed that I had some sort of affection for the rector's Bible; I always sat on it, not because I was religiously inclined, but

52. Cat and a bowl of
goldfish; Victorian
child's picturebook

53. Cat and a bowl of
goldfish by Koryusai,
eighteenth-century

54. The Cat's Dream by Utamaro (1753–1806) (p. 33)

55. Cat chasing a butterfly painted by daughter of Dainagon Yukinari, by Kuniyoshi (1798–1861) (p. 34)

could clearly
distinguish the
words.
"Tell it not to Schippeitaro!
    Keep it close and dark!
Tell it not to
        Schippeitaro!"

A beautiful clear full moon shed its
    light upon this grewsome scene,
        which the young warrior
            watched with
                amaze-
                    ment
                    and
                horror.

            Suddenly, the mid-
                night hour
                being passed,
                the phantom cats

56. Cats dancing; illustration of Japanese tale of Schippeitaro

57. 'Chère Minette', by
Grandville

58. 'Un chat du beau
monde', by Grandville

because it was the only clean spot in the house. She thought that perhaps I might belong to the sect of holy animals, of which Balaam's Ass was an example; so she took me with her.

One morning, I, poor little child of Nature, was attracted by the cream in a bowl, across which lay a muffin. I knocked off the muffin with my paw, and I lapped up the cream; then in my satisfaction and also perhaps as the result of the weakness of my youthful organs, I gave myself up, on the waxed floor, to the most imperious demand experienced by kittens. On perceiving what she called my intemperance and my lack of education, she seized me and beat me soundly with a birch, declaring that she would make a lady of me, or she would abandon me.

'Here's a nice thing,' said she. 'Understand, Miss Beauty, that English cats wrap in the deepest mystery things of Nature which could offend English dignity, and they banish everything that is improper, by applying to the creature, as you have heard the Rev Doctor Simpson say, the laws made by God for the Creation. You must learn to suffer a thousand deaths rather than reveal your desires; it is in this that lies the virtue of Saints. It is the fairest privilege of cats to depart with their characteristic grace, and to go, no one knows whither, to perform their little toilets. You will thus only show yourself when looking your best. Deceived by appearances, everyone will take you for an angel. In future, when seized by a similar desire, you should gaze at the window, with an air of wanting to go for a walk, and then make for the bushes or go into a gutter.'

'And when I am in the gutter?' I thought, gazing at the old lady.

'Once you are alone and sure of being seen by no one, well then, Beauty, you can sacrifice decorum with all the more charm, that you were so much more restrained in public. It is thus that the perfection of English morality shines most clearly, since it is wholly concerned with appearances, this world being, alas, one of appearance and deceit.'

From that moment I habitually hid my favourite tit-bits under beds. No one ever saw me either eating or drinking or making my toilet. I was regarded as a pearl among cats.

When ladies and gentlemen used to pick me up, in order to stroke my back and make the sparks fly from my fur, the maiden lady said with pride: 'You can hold her without the least fear for your dress; she is beautifully brought up!' Everybody said I was an angel, and lavished tit-bits and the most delicate dishes on me; but I declare I was profoundly bored. I understood very well how a young cat in the neighbourhood had come to run away with a tom. This word 'tom' seemed to bring on a sort of sickness in my soul, that nothing would cure, not even the compliments which I received – or rather which my Mistress paid to herself.

'Beauty is completely moral, she is a little angel,' she would say. 'Although she is very lovely, she appears not to be aware of it. She never looks at anyone, which is the very height of the best aristocratic education; it is true that she lets herself be seen very willingly, but she is above all completely unaffected, a quality which we demand of our young girls, but which is very hard to develop. She waits to approach until she is wanted, she never jumps up on you in a familiar manner, no one sees her when she eats, and certainly that monster Lord Byron would have adored her. Like a true Englishwoman she loves tea, sits gravely by when you are explaining the Bible, and thinks evil of no one – and so hears it spoken!'

One evening my Mistress begged one of the young ladies to sing. As soon as this young girl sat down at the piano and began to sing, I immediately recognized the Irish melodies which I had learnt in my childhood, and I realized that I too was a musician. I therefore joined my voice to that of the young girl, but I received an angry smack, whereas the young lady was complimented. This signal act of injustice revolted me, and I took refuge in the attics. Oh sacred love of my country, what a delicious night! I realized what gutters meant. I heard hymns sung by toms to other tabbies, and these adorable elegies made me despise the hypocrisies which my Mistress had forced me to learn. Some of the tabbies then perceived me, and appeared to take umbrage at my presence, when a tom, his fur on end, with a magnificent beard and of a fine bearing, came to look me over, and said to the company, 'It is a child'. At these scornful words, I began to leap on the tiles, and to prance with the agility which distinguishes us, dropping on my paws in that soft and flexible fashion, which no other animal can imitate, in order to prove I was no mere child. But these dainty ways went for nothing. 'When will they sing hymns to me?', I thought to myself. The appearance of these bold toms, their melodies, which no human voice will ever rival, had moved me profoundly, and led me to compose little poems which I sang on the stairs.

But an event of immense importance was about to take place, which tore me away roughly from this innocent existence. I was carried off to London by a niece of my Mistress, a rich heiress, who became crazy about me. She would kiss and pet me in a sort of frenzy, which pleased me so much, that contrary to my usual habit I became attached to her. We were always together, and I was able to observe the best society in London during the Season. It was there that I was to learn about the perversity of English manners, which had spread even to the animals, and to recognize the cant which Lord Byron had denounced, and of which I was a victim as well as he, without having ever published my 'Hours of Idleness'.

Arabella, my Mistress, was a young woman like many others in England; she did not know what sort of husband she wanted. The complete liberty allowed young girls in their choice of a husband drives them almost mad, particularly when they ponder on the stiffness of English manners, which precludes any intimate conversation after marriage. I was far from realizing that the cats of London had adopted this severe code, that English laws would be cruelly applied to me, and that I should undergo sentence at the terrible court of Doctors Commons.

At last one day, an elderly English Peer said to her on seeing me: 'You have a very pretty cat; she is like you, she is white, she is young, she needs a husband; let me introduce to her a magnificent Angora which I have at home'.

Three days later, the Peer brought in the handsomest tom of his lordly house, Puff, black as night, with the most magnificent green and yellow eyes, though cold and proud. His tail, which had yellowish stripes, swept the carpet with its long silky hairs. Perhaps he came from the Imperial House of Austria since he wore, as you perceive, its colours. His manners were those of a cat which had been to Court and lived in the best society. His bearing was so strict, that he would never have scratched his head with his paw, in the presence of anyone. Puff had travelled on the continent. In fine he was so handsome, that the Queen herself had expressed her admiration for him and had actually caressed him. Naively and simply I flung myself round his neck to induce him to play with me. But he refused on the pretext that we were in the presence of other people. I then perceived that this English peer of cats, owing to age and over-eating, had succumbed to that forced and false gravity which the English call respectability. His stoutness, which men admired, hampered his movements. This was the real reason for his refusal to reply to my blandishments; he remained calm and cold, sitting on his posterior, twiddling his whiskers, looking at me and sometimes closing his eyes. In the highest society of English cats, Puff was a splendid match for a cat born in a parsonage; he had two valets to look after him, he ate off Chinese porcelain, he drank tea without milk, he drove in a carriage to Hyde Park, and he attended Parliament.

My Mistress kept him in her house. Unknown to me, the whole feline population of London learnt that Miss Beauty of Catshire was to marry the illustrious Puff, who bore the Austrian colours. During the night I heard a concert in the street; I went down, accompanied by his lordship, who because of his gout, proceeded slowly. We found the cats of the district had come to congratulate me and to beg me to join their Ratophil Society. They explained to me that it was thoroughly common to chase rats and mice. The words 'shocking', 'vulgar', were on every lip. Finally they had formed, for the glory of their country, a Temperance Society. A few nights later, his lordship and I went on the roof at Almack's, to hear a grey cat speak on the question.

'They are our brothers,' he said. And he painted so exquisitely the sufferings of a rat caught in the jaws of a cat, that I was moved to tears. Seeing me the dupe of this speech, Lord Puff told me confidentially that England was hoping for an enormous trade in rats and mice; that if other cats no longer ate them, rats would be cheaper; that behind English morality there was always some economic reason; and that this alliance of morals and commerce was the sole alliance on which England really depended.

Puff seemed to me too much of a politician ever to make a good husband.

My Lord fell asleep. When the Meeting broke up, I heard these delicious words spoken by a young tom from the French Embassy, whose accent proclaimed his nationality:

'Dear Beauty. It will be long before Nature can produce a cat as perfect as you. The cashmeres of Persia and India are like the hides of a camel, compared with your fine and brilliant silk. You breathe a perfume to make Angels swoon with happiness, and I scented it in Prince Talleyrand's drawing-room, which I only left in order to listen to this flood of folly that you call a Meeting. The fire of your eyes lights up the night. Your ears would be perfection itself, if my sighs were to soften them. There is no rose in all England, which is as rosy as the rosy rim of your rosy mouth. A fisherman would search in vain the caverns of Ormus for pearls to rival your teeth. Your dear fine soft muzzle is the prettiest thing produced in England. The Alpine snows would appear brown beside your heavenly coat. Ah, such furs can only be seen in your fogs. Your paws carry softly and gracefully the body which epitomizes the miracles of the Creation; were it not surpassed by your tail, the elegant interpreter of your heart; yes, never did any other cat own a curve so elegant, a rounded shape more perfect, movements more delicate. Abandon this silly old Puff, who goes to sleep like an English Lord in Parliament; besides, the wretch has sold himself to the Whigs, and, through living too long in Bengal, has lost all power to please a lady.'

Without appearing to observe him, I then had a good look at this charming French tom; he was shaggy, small, dashing, not the least like an English cat. His gallant air, as well as the way he shook his ears, proclaimed him a careless rogue. I must confess I was bored by the mere bodily cleanliness of English cats as well as by their solemnity. . . .

However, I woke his lordship and made him understand that it was very late, and that we must go in. I showed no sign of having heard Brisquet's declaration, and my manner appears to have been so frigid that it petrified him. He remained behind, all the more taken aback because he believed himself to be extremely handsome. I learned later that he seduced all tabbies who 'showed willing'. I watched him out of the corner of my eye; he went off in a series of short bounds and came back again in a similar manner, just like a French cat in despair; a true Englishman would have behaved decently and not allowed his feelings to be so obvious. . . .

One night I heard the voice of my French tom in the street. No one could see us; I climbed the chimney and having reached the top of the house, I called out to him: 'To the gutters!' This response lent him wings. He was after me in the twinkling of an eye. Would you believe it? This

French tom had the ill-bred audacity, in reply to my modest little call, to exclaim: 'Come to my paws, darling!' Without any sanction at all, he actually dared to 'darling' me – ME, a cat of distinction!

I looked at him very coldly and, to teach him a lesson, I told him that I belonged to the Temperance Society.

'I see, my dear boy,' I said to him, 'from your accent and the laxity of your principles, that, like most Catholic cats, you are light-minded and would be guilty of a thousand idiocies in the fond belief that you have only to say you're sorry, to get out of the mess. In England, we are more moral; we are respectable in everything, even our pleasures.'

Brisquet was struck dumb by the magnificence of our English cant and listened to me with such close attention that I actually began to hope that I had a convert and that he would become a Protestant cat. He said in a most gentlemanly way, that he would do whatever I wished – provided that I let him adore me! I gazed at him unable to reply; his beautiful, splendid eyes were shining like stars, lighting up the whole night. Encouraged by my silence, he boldly exclaimed: 'Darling Minette!'

'What's this new impertinence?' I cried, though I knew how flippantly French cats talked.

Brisquet explained that on the Continent, everyone, even the King himself, would call his daughter 'Minette, my love!' or 'My little Puss,' as a sign of affection; many women, even the prettiest and most aristocratic, were in the habit of calling their husbands 'Kitten', often even when they were no longer in love with them. If I wanted to make him happy, he said, I would call him 'Manikin'. And upon that he raised his paws with irresistible charm. For fear of yielding to him, I made myself scarce. Brisquet promptly began to sing 'Rule, Britannia!', he was so thrilled; next day, his dear voice was still echoing in my ears.

Meanwhile, a scene was taking place which was to have dreadful consequences for me. Puck, one of Puff's nephews, who had expectations under will and who was living at that time in Wellington Barracks, met my beloved Brisquet. Captain Puck slyly complimented the Attaché on his success with me; according to him, I had resisted all the most charming toms in England. Brisquet, vain Frenchman that he was, said that he would be very happy to attract my attention, although he detested cats who were always talking of temperance and the Bible and such things.

'Aha!' said Puck; 'so she does speak to you!'

My dear French Brisquet had fallen a victim to English diplomacy! And he went on to make one of those idiotic mistakes which outraged all the well-bred tabbies in England. What did the inconsistent young donkey do but greet me in the park and try to talk to me in a familiar manner, as if we knew each other! My instant reaction was to remain cold and distant. The coachman saw Brisquet and gave him a lash with his whip which nearly killed him. Brisquet received the blow without flinching and continued to gaze at me with such courage that my heart was melted. I adored him for seeing only me, while letting himself be beaten and for feeling simply happiness in my presence and for standing his ground in spite of the strong natural instinct of cats to run from the slightest sign of hostility. He did not guess that my outward coldness concealed a feeling that I was going to die. From that moment I made up my mind to elope with him.

That evening on the tiles I threw myself into his arms; I was quite distracted.

'Darling,' I said to him, 'have you enough capital to pay Puff damages?'

'I haven't a bean,' said Brisquet with a laugh, 'except the hairs of my moustache, my four paws and this tail.' And with that he swaggered arrogantly along the gutter.

'No capital!' I exclaimed. 'Why, darling, you're just an adventurer!'

'I dote on adventures!' he said with a languishing look. 'In France, in circumstances like ours, cats spruce themselves up and rely on their claws, not their cash!'

'Poor country! And how on earth do people "without a bean" get assigned to your embassies abroad?'

'Our new government,' said Brisquet, 'isn't interested in its servants' pockets, only in their brains.'

Dear Brisquet's little smirk as he spoke made me think he had too good a conceit of himself.

'It's nonsense to think of love on a shoe-string,' I told him. 'You wouldn't pay much attention to me if you were running about looking for food all the time, my sweet.'

My scamp's only answer was that he was descended on his grandmother's side from Puss-in-Boots. Also, he knew of ninety-nine ways of borrowing money and that we should need only one way of spending it. Finally he said he was musical and could give lessons. And most meltingly he sang me one of his country's national songs, 'Au clair da la lune'.

At this very moment, a number of toms and tabbies, brought along by Puck, caught sight of me just when, overcome by so many arguments, I was promising my beloved Brisquet to follow him anywhere – as soon as he had the means to keep a wife in comfort.

'I'm in for it now,' I groaned.

The very next day, Puff brought an action for 'Criminal conversation' before the Court of Doctors' Commons. Puff was deaf and his nephews traded on it. When they asked him questions, he told them one night I had charmed him by calling him 'Manikin'. This was one of the most damaging accusations against me, as I simply could not explain where I had learnt such an amorous expression. His lordship had without realizing it been my undoing. But then, as I have said before, he was in his second childhood. He had no suspicion of the shabby intrigues of which I was the victim. Several young cats, who did their best to defend me against public opinion, told me that he sometimes asked for his angel, the light of his eyes, his darling, his Beauty. My own Mother, when she came to London, wouldn't see me or listen to me; she said that an English lady cat should be above suspicion, and that I was causing her unhappiness in her old age. My sisters were jealous of my position in Society and sided with my accusers. Even the servants gave evidence against me. I now saw very clearly the sort of situation that made everyone in England lose their heads. The moment there is a question of criminal proceedings, everyone suppresses their natural feelings. A mother is no longer a mother, a nurse repudiates her foster-child, every cat howls in the streets. And what was still more disgusting, my Counsel was won over by Captain Puck – my Counsel, who in his time had actually believed in the innocence of the Queen and to whom I had given every detail. He even assured me that I had nothing to worry about. I thought it was proof of my innocence that I had no idea what the words 'criminal conversation' meant. I told him this and he said that the offence was so named just because it meant nothing but small-talk. Anyhow, the result was that his defence of me was so weak that my cause seemed utterly lost and so I plucked up courage to appear in person before Doctors' Commons.

'My Lords,' said I, 'I am an English cat. I swear that I am innocent. What will they say of the justice of Old England if. . . .' I had scarcely pronounced these words than horrible growls of rage drowned the rest of my speech, so violently had the feelings of the public been aroused by the *Cat-Chronicle* and Puck's friends.

'She is casting doubt on the justice of England, the creator of trial by jury!' they cried.

'She wishes to explain to the Court,' shouted the horrible counsel for the plaintiff, 'how she went on the tiles with a French tom, to convert him to the Anglican Faith, while in fact she went to learn how to say "Manikin" to her unsuspecting husband! To listen to the abominable principles of Popery and to learn to disparage the laws and customs of England!' Well, when the English public hears this sort of farrago of nonsense, it goes potty. Thunders of applause greeted Counsel's words and I was found guilty, at the age of 26 months, although I could prove that I still did not know what a tom was. However, I could now understand why they called England 'Perfidious Albion'.

I fell into a deep hatred of my kind, due less to my divorce than to the death of my beloved Brisquet. Puck had had him killed in a riot, thinking he might try to take his revenge. Besides, nothing infuriated me more than to hear people boasting of the loyalty of English cats.

And so you see, Animals of France, what happens when we get to know men; we copy their vices and adopt their evil institutions. Let us go back to the wilds, where we shall follow only our own instincts and where customs are not opposed to the holy dictates of nature. . . .

I forgot to tell you that although Brisquet had a bullet wound in his back, the revolting hypocrite of a Coroner 'found' that he had poisoned himself with arsenic – as if a tom, so gay, so crazy, so scatter-brained could ever have reflected on life enough to have entertained such a serious idea. How *could* a cat whom *I* loved ever have had the faintest desire to quit this life?

True, – or is it? – they found stains on a plate, by using **Marsh's** apparatus . . . .

from *Peines de Coeur d'une Chatte Anglaise*
by Honoré de Balzac, tr. by May Elizabeth Jenkin

'A singular creature', by Grandville

Letters from Minette to Bébé

'I was unhappy,' wrote Minette in her third letter to Bébé, 'and he [Brisquet] guaranteed, by written contract, that I should enjoy unclouded happiness. I should never know sorrow, I should shine like a diamond. I should be envied by every Tabby in France; in short, I should be his wife, the Ambassadress's cat, and bear a title.

What can I say, Bébé, I just *had* to follow him, and that is how I became MADAME BRISQUET.'

Alas, Brisquet is faithless and deserts Minette. She describes it in her fourth letter:

'It was only natural, then, that while Brisquet was forgetting me he was already smitten with another charmer.

'As luck would have it my rival was a singular creature, a Chinese cat from the province of Pechy-Ly, who had only just arrived and already had all the Tom Cats of Paris – those notorious gadabouts, running after her.

'It was just at this time that the remarkable story about the disappearance of Brisquet, *The Love Affairs of an English Cat,* was written. It is a charming novel, no doubt, but also the most appalling tissue of lies you can possibly imagine, and all the worse because it contains a grain of truth. It was at Brisquet's instigation that this story was written by a distinguished author whose credulity he contrived to abuse (for nobody could resist his blandishments) by persuading him to believe and write whatever he wanted.

'By giving out that he was dead, Brisquet hoped to obtain his freedom and marry this Chinese creature while I was still alive – in short, to commit bigamy! This he accomplished in defiance of all laws, both human and divine, by assuming another name.

'It would indeed be quite easy to refute this baseless English tale, which originated solely in the lively imagination of Brisquet and his writer of romances. The events it purports to relate could never have taken place in England, where no action for *crim. con.* was ever brought before Doctors' Commons, and where no injured husband ever petitioned the courts, except for *money* – and to cure him of a broken heart.'

Poor Minette fell ill and in her eighth letter to Bébé she tells how her mistress has decided to have her drowned:

'As I write this letter to you, Bébé, the housemaid whom my noble mistress [the Ambassador's wife] had made my personal attendant, is sewing up a grey canvas bag. When three sides have been sewn up I shall be put in the bag, the fourth side will be sewn up and I shall be handed over to the first footman who will carry me to the Pont Neuf and throw me into the water. Such is to be my fate.

'Goodbye, Bébé, just a few more minutes, just a few more stitches, and that will be the end of me. I shall die without kissing you all for the last time.'

But Minette is *not* drowned. An epilogue recounts how both the Ambassadress and the maid died suddenly and mysteriously before the bag was completely sewn up.

Soon after this she heard of the death of Brisquet who was thrown into the street from the fourth storey of a house by a husband whom he had wronged.

Minette rejoins Bébé and decides to remain a widow.

'You only love once,' she said.

She lived happily with Bébé and Bébé's husband and 'the only unhappy people were the unfortunate cats who sighed and still sigh for her'.

from *Poor Minette* by Julian Jacobs, from the French of P.-J. Stahl

Minette, by Grandville

The story of Sylvia

Sandy Wilson's 'Sylvia' is a modern Minette and her autobiography *This Is Sylvia* is graced by the author's own delightfully witty illustrations Their economy of line perhaps appeals more to modern taste than Grandville's more elaborate style, but they are in the same satirical tradition.

Sylvia embarks on her stage career soon after her mother has run off to California with an American 'Big Business Boss' cat, named Cyrus T. Rocksalmonfeller. She is given her first big chance to play a leading lady, or cat, by Laurence Fortescue who had just written and composed a new operetta while on holiday in the Bahamas.

'He was a delight to work with,' writes Sylvia, 'and all the cast adored him. I know that nowadays he is considered somewhat of a period piece, but at the time I knew him he was at the height of his powers, and I think it is generally agreed that his music and lyrics for *That Old Fragrance* were among the best he ever wrote.'

Later, Sylvia goes, of course, to Hollywood, where, after a series of successes in the Goldfisch Studios, she cuts out a star named Miaow-Miaow Latouche in a love-affair with a millionaire oil magnate, Blackie Diabolo.

Laurence Fortescue, by Sandy Wilson

'. . . I found myself standing next to an extremely handsome black cat, who was, of course, Mr Diabolo. He offered me a cigarette, and the next thing I knew a flash bulb exploded in our faces. I thought nothing of it at the time; but the next morning, to my horror, I found that the picture was in the paper over a typical piece of Nellie Nipper's gossip, headlined, "Look out, Miaow-Miaow! Sylvia's moving in!"'

Presently, Sylvia is on the Riviera with Blackie, but her affair with him doesn't last long. Blackie was arrested for various swindles. Sylvia goes off to Italy where she meets a number of people prominent in society and in the literary world, among them the easily recognizable Pandora Tickell.

'I found Pandora Tickell a most unusual person. Her taste in clothes was quite bizarre and she would wander round the villa and its gardens looking like an evocation of the Italian Renaissance. . . . From time to time Pandora Tickell would rise and declaim passages from her new cycle of poems, 'The Chaffinch and the Cod', most of which I'm afraid I found a little obscure.'

Eventually, Sylvia comes home, marries Sir Algernon Gutts-Whyting, divorces him, marries again and lives happily ever after.

'Blackie and I in the South of France', by Sandy Wilson

Crumwhull's Gibb Cat

In Gallowa now some hae heard
  O' Auld Crumwhull's Gibb Cat,
Or may be no – the de'il the odds,
  Let bards alane for that –
And there's o' them wad rather hear
  About ane big Gibb Cat,
As o' the grandest richest king
  On gowden throne ere sat –

Or warrier faeming on a naig,
  Owre blude besumped fields,
There splitting pows – there jagging hearts,
  And jingling on shields –
Or statesmen thumping ither down,
  Wi' a' the pith o' chat,
Ane nobler theme than them by far
  Is Auld Crumwhull's Gibb Cat –

Wha worried ance a fumart dead,
  And shook him after hin,
Wha did the girnell o' Crumwhull
  O' rattons aften thin –
Wha crumpet mice like raisings up,
  And mony anither thing,
Wha aft upo' the knee wad loup
  O' Auld Crumwhull and sing –

For Auld Crumwhull wad straik his back,
  And ane sleek grey back had he;
Than wad he cock his tail fu' straught,
  And nyurr awa wi' glee –
He lo'ed the auld man unco weel,
  For why he used him sae,
As selfishness had the Gibb Cat,
  And men the same whiles hae –

Ay, ay, the maist o' mankind hae
  Enough atweel o' that,

There's some o' them mair selfish far
    Than ony grey Gibb Cat –
Wha seem to sing a friendly sang,
    And act a friendly part,
But hoh anee their sellie tugs,
    Warst at the rotten heart –

Frae death's door nane they wad relieve,
    Tho' that was in their power,
Unless fu' sure they wad be paid
    For doin't ten times owre –
What think they, no' that they'll see heaven,
    O! sure they can't think that;
For heaven they'll never, never, see,
    Mair than Crumwhull's Gibb Cat –

Wha ne'er had ony thought to lae,
    The kind place o' Crumwhull,
Mair than to lae the ocean has
    Ane keckling sea-gull –
But Auld Crumwhull, through perfect age,
    Was ta'en to his lang hame,
Sae his bien ha' and a' his lands
    Anither laird's became –

Wha brought fell tykes about the house,
    Whilk had nae sense ava,
For they did hunt the gude Gibb Cat,
    Frae dear Crumwhull awa –
He ran tae wuds, and lived upon
    Young gorbs which he did fin'
In burdies' nests and ither things,
    Which sleekened his skin –

There turned a wullcat true did he,
    Ane mad and furious pest,
And sleepit ay on taps o' trees,
    In some snug corbie's nest –
The boys wha used to roam that wud,
    And gather leaming nits,
Wad sometimes by the fell Gibb Cat,
    Been flung in fearfu' fits –

They heard him myauing mony a time,
    Whan de'il the myau gaed he,

And saw him too, whar he was not,
  For what won't terror see –
And whan a mither wanted whiles,
  Her squaching bairnie gude,
She'd fley'd frae greeting a' at ance,
  Wi' the wullcat o' the wud –

Nae witch e'er wond in Binwood glen,
  Was sic a fount o' fear,
Nae gaunting ghaist in auld kirkyard,
  Made sic a tale sae drear –
Nor need we wonder at the thing,
  For flaming grew his e'en,
And mair than that he grew a cat,
  The like was never seen –

Thus thrave the awsome Gibb for years,
  What bawdrons was like him?
What puss had e'er his whusking tail,
  Or yet his strength o' lim'?
Ane winter time, lang lay the snaw
  Twa gude ell deep and mair,
Whilk pat *Sir Gibbie* to his wits,
  For food wharon to fare –

He kend a farmer just hard by,
  Made aften sweet milk cheese,
And raw'd them nicely on his deals,
  As *yallow* as ye please –
Af in a bonny moonlight night,
  Ran the grimalkin there,
Broke through the wunnock in a crack,
  And on them sweet did fare –

He broke the *scroof* o' three or four,
  And left them sad to see
By the gude wife at scregh o' day,
  And mad as she cud be –
Revenge was vow'd wi' mony a curse,
  Against the thief unkend,
The next night they wad sit and watch,
  And try his tricks to mend –

Wi' swooples, spurkles, beetles, fows,
  The family a' war arm'd,

And haith they faun' use for them a',
   For they war sair alarm'd –
Whan in cam spanging to the cheese,
   The hule and wha was that,
Lord save our sauls, they yelloch'd a',
   It is Crumwhull's Gibb Cat –

By the chulders he seized on the gudewife,
   And soon wad hae stap'd her breath,
Had na her man, her sons and daughters,
   Barried him to death –
A wee thing didna kill the chiel,
   He fuff'd, he bit, and spat,
Sae merry Scotsmen now ye'll ken
   About Crumwhull's Gibb Cat –

Tho' for the moral o' the tale,
   Let nane that moral tell –
May every birkie watch his saul,
   And haud it out o' hell.

Old Galloway Ballad

Glossary of words in order of appearance

Gibb Cat *male cat*
faeming *foaming*
naig *nag*
besumped *drenched*
pows *heads*
fumart *pole-cat*
girnell *meal chest*
rattons *rats*
crumpet *crunched*
raisings *raisins*
nyurr *purr*
hoh anee their sellie tugs *alas, their self rules them*
lae *leave*
bien *snug*
tykes *dogs*
gorbs *fledglings*
wullcat *wildcat*
corbie *crow*

leaming *shining*
nits *nuts*
squaching *squalling*
fley'd *frightened*
greeting *crying*
wond in *haunted*
bawdrons *cat*
raw'd *put out in rows*
wunnock *window*
scroof *crust*
skregh *break*
unkend *unknown*
swoople *business end of a flail*
spurkles *sticks*
beetles *mallets*
fows *pitchforks*
hule *hell*
chulders *double-chin*
birkie *fellow*

59. *Above:* The Cat Family at Home, by Kuniyoshi (p. 34)
60. *Below:* Cats dancing, by Kuniyoshi

61. Cat dancing to Witch-Cat, Kuniyoshi (p. 34 and p. 41)

62. Cat and witch, Kuniyoshi (p. 34)

63. Faces of cat-actors, Kuniyoshi (p. 34)

The law of the cat

Extracts from the Codes enacted by Howel the Good (Hywel Dda) Prince of South Wales, circa A.D. 940

This is the complement of a lawful hamlet: nine buildings and one plough and one kiln and one churn and one cat and one cock and one bull and one herdman.

The animals whose tail, eyes and life are of equal worth: a calf, a filly from common work and a cat, excepting the cat that shall watch the King's barn.

Whoever shall catch a cat mousing in his flax garden, let its owner pay the damage.

The Vendotian (or North Wales) code

The worth of a cat and her teithi is this:

1. The worth of a kitten from the night it is kittened until it shall open its eyes is a legal penny.
2. And from that time, until it shall kill mice, two legal pence.
3. And after it shall kill mice, four legal pence; and so it always remains.
4. Her teithi are, to see, to hear, to kill mice, to have her claws entire, to rear and not to devour her kittens; and if she be bought, and be deficient in any one of those teithi, let one-third of her worth be returned.

The Gwentian or South-east code

1. Whoever shall kill a cat that guards a house and a barn of the King, or shall take it stealthily, it is to be held with its head to the ground and its tail up, the ground being swept, and then clean wheat is to be poured about it, until the tip of its tail be hidden; and that is its worth.
2. Another cat is four legal pence in value.
3. The teithi of a cat are, that it be perfect of ear, perfect of eye, perfect of

teeth, perfect of tail, perfect of claw and without marks of fire; and that it will kill mice well; and that it shall not devour its kittens; and that it be not caterwauling on every new moon.

4. The teithi and the legal worth of a cat are co-equal.

5. A pound is the worth of a pet animal of the king.

6. The pet animal of a breyr is six score pence in value.

7. The pet animal of a taeog is a curt penny in value.

Glossary

teithi *the qualities or attributes of the cat*
breyr *a class of freeman*
taeog *a class of husbandman*

A Welsh church cat

As I and my family sat at tea in our parlour, an hour or two after we had taken possession of our lodgings, the door of the room and that of the entrance of the house being open, on account of the fineness of the weather, a poor black cat entered hastily, sat down on the carpet by the table, looked up towards us, and mewed piteously. I had never seen so wretched a looking creature. It was dreadfully attenuated, being little more than skin and bone, and was sorely afflicted with an eruptive malady.

And here I may as well relate the history of this cat previous to our arrival which I subsequently learned by bits and snatches. It had belonged to a previous vicar of Llangollen, and had been left behind at his departure. His successor brought with him dogs and cats who conceiving that the late vicar's cat had no business at the vicarage, drove it forth to seek another home, which, however, it could not find. Almost all the people of the suburb were dissenters, as indeed were the generality of the people at Llangollen, and knowing the cat to be a church cat, not only would not harbour it, but did all they could to make it miserable; whilst the few who were not dissenters, would not receive it into their houses, either because they had cats of their own, or dogs, or did not want a cat, so that the cat had no home and was dreadfully persecuted by nine-tenths of the suburb. Oh, there never was a cat so persecuted as that poor Church of England animal, and solely on account of the opinions which it was supposed to have imbibed in the house of its late master, for I never could learn that the dissenters of the suburb, nor indeed of Llangollen in general, were in the habit of persecuting other cats; the cat was a Church of England cat, and that was enough: stone it, hang it, drown it! were the cries of almost everybody. If the workmen of the flannel factory, all of whom were Calvinistic Methodists, chanced to get a glimpse of it in the road from the windows of the building, they would sally forth in a body, and with sticks, stones, or for want of other weapons, with clots of horse-dung, of which there was always plenty on the road, would chase it up the high bank or perhaps over the Camlas – the inhabitants of a small street between our house and the factory leading from the road to the river, all of whom were dissenters, if they saw it moving about the perllan, into which their back windows looked, would shriek and hoot at it, and fling anything of no value which came easily to hand, at the head or body of the ecclesiastical cat. The good woman of the house, who though a very excellent person, was a bitter dissenter, whenever she saw it upon her ground or heard it was there, would make after it, frequently attended by her maid Margaret, and her young son, a boy about nine years of age, both of whom hated the cat, and were always ready to attack it, either alone or in company, and no wonder, the maid being not only a dissenter, but a class teacher, and the boy not only a dissenter, but intended for the dissenting ministry. Where it got its food and food it sometimes must have got, for even a cat, an animal known to have nine lives, cannot live without food, was only known to itself, as was the place where it lay, for even a cat must lie down sometimes; though a labouring man who occasionally dug in the garden told me he believed that in the spring time it ate freshets, and the woman of the house once said that she believed it sometimes slept in the hedge, which hedge, by the bye, divided our perllan from the vicarage grounds, which were very extensive.

Well might the cat having led this kind of life for better than two years look mere skin and bone when it made its appearance in our apartment, and have an eruptive malady, and also a bronchitic cough, for I remember it had both. How it came to make its appearance there is a mystery, for it had never entered the house before, even when there were lodgers; that it should not visit the woman who was its declared enemy, was natural enough, but why if it did not visit her other lodgers did it visit us? Did instinct keep it aloof from them? Did instinct draw it towards us? We gave it some bread and butter, and a little tea with milk and sugar. It ate and drank and soon began to purr.

The good woman of the house was horrified when on coming in to remove the things she saw the church cat on her carpet. 'What impudence!' she exclaimed, and made towards it, but on our telling her that we did not expect that it should be disturbed, she let it alone. A very remarkable circumstance was, that though the cat had hitherto been in the habit of flying not only from her face, but the very echo of her voice, it now looked her in the face with perfect composure, as much as to say 'I don't fear you, for I know that I am now safe and with my own people'. It stayed with us two hours and then went away. The next morning it returned. To be short, though it went away every night, it became our own cat, and one of our family. I gave it something which cured it of its eruption, and through good treatment it soon lost its other ailments and began to look sleek and bonny.

We were at first in some perplexity with respect to the disposal of the ecclesiastical cat; it would of course not do to leave it in the garden to the tender mercies of the Calvinistic Methodists of the neighbourhood, more especially those of the flannel manufactory, and my wife and daughter could hardly carry it with them. At length we thought of applying to a young woman of sound church principles who was lately married and lived over the water on the way to the railway station, with whom we were slightly acquainted, to take charge of the animal, and she on the first intimation of our wish willingly acceded to it. So with her poor puss was left along with a trifle for its milk money, and with her, as we subsequently learned, it continued in peace and comfort till one morning it sprang suddenly from the hearth into the air, gave a mew and died.

So much for the ecclesiastical cat.

from *Wild Wales* by George Borrow

On the death of a favourite cat drowned in a tub of gold-fishes

'Twas on a lofty vase's side.
Where China's gayest art had dyed
   The azure flowers that blow,
Demurest of the tabby kind,
The pensive Selima, reclined,
   Gazed on the lake below.

Her conscious tail her joy declared;
The fair round face, the snowy beard,
   The velvet of her paws,
Her coat that with the tortoise vies,
Her ears of jet, and emerald eyes,
   She saw, and purred applause.

Still had she gazed, but 'midst the tide,
Two angel forms were seen to glide –
   The Genii of the stream:
Their scaly armour's Tyrian hue,
Through richest purple, to the view
   Betrayed a golden gleam.

The hapless nymph with wonder saw:
A whisker first, and then a claw,
   With many an ardent wish,
She stretched in vain to reach the prize:
What female heart can gold despise?
   What cat's averse to fish?

Presumptuous maid! with looks intent,
Again she stretched, again she bent,
   Nor knew the gulf between.
Malignant Fate sat by and smiled:
The slippery verge her feet beguiled;
   She stumbled headlong in.

Eight times emerging from the flood,
She mewed to every watery god
   Some speedy aid to send.
No Dolphin came, no Nereid stirred,
Nor cruel Tom or Susan heard;
   A favourite has no friend!

From hence, ye Beauties! undeceived,
Know one false step is ne'er retrieved,
   And be with caution bold:
Not all that tempts your wandering eyes
And heedless hearts is lawful prize,
   Nor all that glisters, gold.

Thomas Gray

A cat's prayer

Lord,
I am the cat.
It is not, exactly, that I have something to ask of You
No –
I ask nothing of anyone –
but,
if You have by some chance, in some celestial barn,
a little white mouse,
or a saucer of milk,
I know someone who would relish them.
Wouldn't You like someday
to put a curse on the whole race of dogs?
If so, I should say,
                    Amen

from *Prayers from the Ark*
by Bernos de Gasztold tr. Rumer Godden

64. 'The Last Supper'; 17th century tiles, Womersley Church, Yorkshire (p. 42)

65. Pair of cloisonné cats; sixteenth century Chinese

66. Cat with kittens by Gottfried Mind (p. 33)
67. Cat and mouse by Gottfried Mind (p. 33)

Salutation and cat

It had been discovered that for twenty-five years past an oral addition to the written standing orders of the native guard at Government House, near Poona, had been communicated regularly from one guard to another, on relief, to the effect that any cat passing out of the front door after dark was to be regarded as His Excellency the Governor, and to be saluted accordingly. The meaning of this was that Sir Robert Grant, Governor of Bombay, had died there in 1838, and on the evening of the day of his death, a cat was seen to leave the house by the front door and walk up and down a particular path, as had been the Governor's habit to do, after sunset. A Hindu sentry had observed this and he mentioned it to others of his faith, who made it a subject of superstitious conjecture, the result being that one of the priestly class explained the mystery of the dogma of the transmigration of the soul from one body to another, and interpreted the circumstances to mean that the spirit of the deceased Governor had entered into one of the House pets. It was difficult to fix on a particular one, and it was therefore decided that every cat passing out of the main entrance after dark was to be regarded as the tabernacle of Governor Grant's soul, and to be treated with due respect and the proper honours. This decision was accepted without question by all the native attendants and others belonging to Government House.

The whole guard from sepoy to subahdar fully acquiesced in it, and an oral addition was made to the standing orders that the sentry at the front door would 'present arms' to any cat passing out there after dark. The notion was essentially Hindu, yet the Mahomedans and the native Christians and Jews (native Jews are to be found in the Bombay army) devoutly assented to it. Dread of the supernatural overcame all religious objections, and everyone bowed scrupulously to the heathen decree.

from *A Varied Life* by Sir Thomas Gordon (1832–1914)

Archibald Bell-the-Cat

James III, King of Scotland, is described by Sir Walter Scott in *Tales of a Grandfather* as 'an unwise and unwarlike prince'. During his reign, he caused his brother, the Earl of Mar, to be murdered and later granted the revenues and title of the Earldom to Robert Cochran, a mason, who had become the King's principal favourite.

In the year 1482, there was prospect of imminent war with England and the King collected a great army at Lauder, some twenty-five miles from Edinburgh. The great barons, however, were, as Scott tells us, 'less disposed to advance against the English, than to correct the abuses of the King's administration'.

He proceeds:

'Many of the nobility and barons held a secret council in the church of Lauder, where they enlarged upon the evils which Scotland sustained through the insolence and corruption of Cochran and his associates. While they were thus declaiming, Lord Gray requested their attention to a fable. "The mice," he said, "being much annoyed by the persecution of the cat, resolved that a bell should be hung about puss's neck, to give notice when she was coming. But though the measure was agreed to in full council, it could not be carried into effect, because no mouse had courage enough to undertake to tie the bell to the neck of the formidable enemy." This was as much as to intimate his opinion, that though the discontented nobles might make bold resolutions against the King's ministers, yet it would be difficult to find anyone courageous enough to act upon them.

'Archibald, Earl of Angus, a man of gigantic strength and intrepid courage, and head of that second family of Douglas whom I before mentioned, started up when Gray had done speaking. "I am he," he said, "who will bell the cat;" from which expression he was distinguished by the name of Bell-the-Cat to his dying day.

'While thus engaged, a loud authoritative knocking was heard at the door of the church. This announced the arrival of Cochran, attended by a guard of three hundred men, attached to his own person, and all gaily dressed in his livery of white, with black facings, and armed with partisans.

'As Cochran entered the church, Angus, to make good his promise to bell the cat, met him, and rudely pulled the gold chain from his neck, saying "A halter would better become him".'

(Cochran was later hanged from the centre of Lauder bridge.)

from *Tales of a Grandfather* by Sir Walter Scott

The master's cat

One evening we were all, except father, going to a ball, and when we started, we left 'the master' and his cat in the drawing-room together. 'The Master' was reading at a small table; suddenly the candle went out. My father, who was much interested in his book, relighted the candle, stroked the cat, who was looking at him pathetically he noticed, and continued his reading. A few minutes later, as the light became dim, he looked up just in time to see puss deliberately put out the candle with his paw, and then look appealingly at him. This second and unmistakable hint was not disregarded and puss was given the petting he craved.

from *My Father as I Recall Him*
(by Mary, daughter of Charles Dickens)

Sam Weller and Mr Brooks's cats

'I lodged in the same house vith a pieman once, sir, and a wery nice man he was – reg'lar clever chap, too – make pies out o' anything, he could. "What a number o' cats you keep, Mr Brooks," says I, when I'd got intimate with him. "Ah," says he, "I do – a good many," says he. "You must be wery fond o' cats," says I. "Other people is," says he, a-winkin' at me; "they ain't in season till the winter though," says he. "Not in season!" says I. "No," says he, "fruits is in, cats is out." "Why, what do you mean?" says I. "Mean?" says he. "That I'll never be a party to the combination o' the butchers, to keep up the price o' meat," says he. "Mr Weller," says he, a-squeezing my hand wery hard, and vispering in my ear – "don't mention this here agin – but it's the seasonin' as does it. They're all made o' them noble animals," says he, a-pointin' to a wery nice little tabby kitten, "and I seasons 'em for beefsteak, weal, or kidney, 'cording to the demand. And more than that," says he, "I can make a weal a beef-steak, or a beef-steak a kidney, or any one on 'em a mutton, at a minute's notice, just as the market changes, and appetites wary!" '

'He must have been a very ingenious young man, that, Sam,' said Mr Pickwick, with a slight shudder.

from *The Pickwick Papers* by Charles Dickens

Mrs Forrester's lace

. . . I treasure up my lace very much. . . . I always wash it myself. And
once it had a narrow escape. Of course, your ladyship knows that such
lace must never be starched or ironed. Some people wash it in sugar and
water, and some in coffee, to make it the right yellow colour; but I
myself have a very good receipt for washing it in milk, which stiffens it
enough and gives it a very good creamy colour. Well, ma'am, I had
tacked it together (and the beauty of this fine lace is that, when it is wet,
it goes into a very little space), and put it to soak in milk, when, unfortunately, I left the room; on my return I found pussy on the table, looking
very like a thief, but gulping very uncomfortably, as if she was half-choked
with something she wanted to swallow and could not. And would you
believe it? At first I pitied her, and said 'Poor pussy! Poor pussy!' till, all
at once, I looked and saw the cup of milk empty – cleaned out! 'You
naughty cat!' said I; and I believe I was provoked enough to give her a
slap, which did no good, but only helped the lace down – just as one slaps
a choking child on the back. I could have cried, I was so vexed; but I
determined I would not give the lace up without a struggle for it. I hoped
the lace might disagree with her, at any rate; but it would have been too
much for Job, if he had seen, as I did, that cat come in, quite placid and
purring, not a quarter of an hour after, and almost expecting to be
stroked. 'No, pussy!' said I, 'if you have any conscience you ought not to
expect that!' And then a thought struck me; and I rang the bell for my
maid, and sent her to Mr Hoggins, with my compliments, and would he
be kind enough to lend me one of his top-boots for an hour? I did not
think there was anything odd in the message; but Jenny said the young
men in the surgery laughed as if they would be ill at my wanting a top-
boot. When it came, Jenny and I put pussy in, with her fore-feet straight
down, so that they were fastened, and could not scratch, and we gave her
a teaspoonful of currant-jelly in which (your ladyship must excuse me) I
had mixed some tartar emetic. I shall never forget how anxious I was for
the next half-hour. I took pussy to my own room, and spread a clean
towel on the floor. I could have kissed her when she returned the lace to
sight, very much as it had gone down. Jenny had boiling water ready, and
we soaked it and soaked it, and spread it on a lavender-bush in the sun
before I could touch it again, even to put it in milk. But now your
ladyship would never guess that it had been in pussy's inside.

from *Cranford* by Mrs Gaskell

Nine lives

Being, at this moment, something out of humour with life, I envy most my cat. Of all my friends, she is the wisest. She is sixty miles away from where I sit here writing. Still I know well how it is with her. That little half-hour of sun has found her stretched out upon a wickerwork seat under the old vine that is southward of my house.

Her fur was warm in it and keeps yet the warmth. She is content. They have brought her milk and she has lapped it slowly, tasting it with each lap of the tongue, not hastening as do cats that are houseless, and without service. After this break of the fast she has washed herself from ears to tail, deliberately, with nice ceremony, like a priestess who must go clean of body to the holy rites. And then, I know, she took the sun and eased every limb in that mild light. Her yellow eyes blink; she is deep in comfortable meditation. She is very wise, but not in our troublesome wisdom. For in the passing of her nine lives she learned how to live.

That every pussy has nine lives is a truth not to be questioned. I have never doubted it, although it be a hard saying and mysterious. For if you tell the cat's years as we number ours, pussy's life seems but a span-long life, very short and soon to pass. It is not well with us who love to have the most companionable of all beasts near to us for sympathy. They go but a little way with us and then leave us. It is not good for us to measure life by the deaths of so many friends; I am not yet comforted for the death of the pussy who, when I wrote, loved to keep very near to me, lying across my shoulder.

And yet, though in the sight of men they seem to hasten away, the truth is in that old wisdom. We have but one life and they have nine, a taste of the leisures of immortality. I think that in their short years they lived out the nine, serenely, graciously, without care and hastening. Care, says the proverb, once killed a cat. It may be so, but it has killed never another.

Pussy was a goddess in old Egypt, and she has never forgotten it. Old incense perfumes her soft fur. A goddess in exile, she exacts honour as any queen who has lost a realm but will have her court and its courtiers. Obedience is strange to her. All the tribe of dog may be at your command; pussycat must not be commanded, but entreated. For this I love her and company with her, not loving to have any but an equal near me in the privacy of my room. We are of the same mood, she and I.

We lie under the same condemnation. We have the same liking for long leisure, the meditative humour, and there are those who will call us lazy in the grain of us. We are both inapt for any toil, although I, who am under the curse of Adam, who am not of the divine stock, must sadly labour for the pair of us and for the bread of all those who in my house do service and worship in the cat.

There is a foolish legend that the catching of mice is a cat's duty, her share of the world's work. It is true that she catches them; one was brought to me yesterday and dropped on the hearthrug by a cat who has a sportsmanlike vanity and would be praised and called a hunting Diana. But this is not work, the census-taker does not put the slayer of pheasants beside the bricklayer and the journalist, as a toiler among the toilers. A saddle for the horse and a collar for the house dog. If the cat waits for long hours, silent beside the crack of the wainscot, it is for pure pleasure. Cats do not keep the mice away; it is my belief that they preserve them for the chase.

She has nine lives because she can spend well one life that runs between the hour when mewling, blind, she is newborn in a basket, and the hour when she will die, simply and decently; without fear or regret like a cat. She has warmed all four paws by the fire of life, and, when the time comes, will be ready to depart. All her desires have been fulfilled in living; the long hours of basking idleness have brought her the last wisdom. Enviously, I think it might be so with me if life were less cumbered with foolish business.

I will compare her with the Buddhist who goes apart from his fellows to meditate upon the Way. But the Buddhist cuts a pitiful figure when you compare him with pussy. He must go out and away and be alone, enduring hardness before he can begin his thinking. My admirable cat has never denied herself one of the little pleasures of life. She eats delicately, will have her milk of the newest; tells me, clawing gently at my knee, that she is eager for fish. She will lie soft at night, and, by day, will take the sun as though it shone for her; she dreams happily by the winter fire. Yet if the Buddhist, in his long meditation, touched at the limit of wisdom and came to that boundary wall which marks the last marches of knowledge, he will find that my cat is there before, is there upon the wall, looking down on him, blinking yellow eyes in pity upon the poor man who has been vexed by his dream of life beyond life in wearisome reincarnations. She knows that nine lives are enough and that sleep is good.

from *Day In and Day Out*
by Oswald Barron, F.S.A. (Author and Antiquary. 1868–1939)

It has been the providence of nature to give this creature nine lives instead of one. *Fables of Bidpai*

Cats have nine lives, onions and women seven skins. *Proverb*

To a cat which had killed a favourite bird

O Cat in semblance, but in heart akin
To canine raveners, whose ways are sin;
Still at my hearth a guest thou dar'st to be?
Unwhipt of Justice, hast no dread of me?
Or deem'st the sly allurements shall avail
Of purring throat and undulating tail?
No! as to pacify Patroclus dead
Twelve Trojans by Pelides' sentence bled,
So shall thy blood appease the feathery shade,
And for one guiltless life shall nine be paid.

Richard Garnett (after Agathias 536–82)

Tama's dream kittens

Very much do I love cats; and I suppose that I could write a large book about the different cats which I have kept, in various climes and times on both sides of the world. But this is not a Book of Cats; and I am writing about Tama for merely psychological reasons. She has been uttering, in her sleep beside my chair, a peculiar cry that touched me in a particular way. It is the cry that a cat makes only for her kittens, – a soft trilling coo, – a pure caress of tone. And I perceive that her attitude, as she lies there on her side, is the attitude of a cat holding something, – something freshly caught; the forepaws are stretched out as to grasp, and the pearly talons are playing.

We call her Tama ('Jewel') – not because of her beauty, though she is beautiful, but because Tama is a female name accorded by custom to pet cats. She was a very small tortoise-shell kitten when she was first brought to me as a gift worth accepting, – a cat-of-three-colours (*miké neto*) being somewhat uncommon in Japan. In certain parts of the country such a cat is believed to be a luck-bringer, and gifted with power to frighten away goblins as well as rats. Tama is now two years old. I think that she has foreign blood in her veins: she is more graceful and more slender than the ordinary Japanese cat; and she has a remarkably long tail, which, from a Japanese point of view, is her only defect. Perhaps one of her ancestors came to Japan in some Dutch, or Spanish ship during the time of Iyeyasu. But, from whatever ancestors descended, Tama is quite a Japanese cat in her habits; – for example, she eats rice!

The first time that she had kittens, she proved herself an excellent mother – devoting all her strength and intelligence to the care of her little ones, until, by dint of nursing them and moiling for them, she became piteously and ludicrously thin. She taught them how to keep clean, – how to play and jump and wrestle, – how to hunt. At first, of course, she gave them only her long tail to play with; and later she found them other toys. She brought them not only rats and mice, but also frogs, lizards, a bat, and one day a small lamprey, which she must have managed to catch in a neighbouring rice-field. After dark I used to leave open for her a small window at the head of the stairs leading to my study, – in order that she might go out to hunt by way of the kitchen roof. And one night she brought in through that window a big straw sandal for her kittens to play with. She found it in the field; and she must have carried it over a wooden fence ten feet high, up the house wall to the roof of the kitchen, and thence through the bars of the little window to the stairway. There she and her

137

kittens played boisterously with it till morning; and they dirtied the stairway, for that sandal was muddy. Never was cat more fortunate in her first maternal experience than Tama. But the next time she was not fortunate. She had got into the habit of visiting friends in another street, at a perilous distance; and one evening, while on her way thither, she was hurt by some brutal person. She came back to us stupid and sick; and her kittens were born dead. I thought that she would die also; but she recovered much more quickly than anybody could have imagined possible, – though she still remains, for obvious reasons, troubled in spirit by the loss of the kittens.

The memory of animals, in regard to certain forms of relative experience, is strangely weak and dim. But the organic memory of the animal, – the memory of experience accumulated through countless millions of lives, – is superhumanly vivid, and very seldom at fault. . . . Think of the astonishing skill with which a cat can restore the respiration of her drowned kitten! Think of her untaught ability to face a dangerous enemy seen for the first time, – a venomous serpent, for example! Think of her wide experience with small creatures and their ways, – her medical knowledge of herbs, – her capacities of strategy, whether for hunting or fighting! What she knows is really considerable; and she knows it all perfectly, or almost perfectly. But it is the knowledge of other existences. Her memory, as to the pains of her present life, is mercifully brief.

Tama could not clearly remember that her kittens were dead. She knew that she ought to have had kittens; and she looked everywhere and called everywhere for them, long after they had been buried in the garden. She complained a great deal to her friends; and she made me open all the cupboards and closets, – over and over again, – to prove to her that the kittens were not in the house. At last she was able to convince herself that it was useless to look for them any more. But she plays with them in dreams, and coos to them, and catches for them small shadowy things, – perhaps even brings to them, through some dim window of memory, a sandal of ghostly straw. . . .

from *Kottō* by Lafcadio Hearn

138

The city of the cats

The Dog gives himself the Airs of a Cat. Richard Steele

The City of the Cats was beautiful. Even the Dogs were aware of its fantastic beauty. It stood near the head of a valley at the point where a grey cataract of rocks was giving way to a level bottom striped with meadows. In these fertile meadows grazed the herds of creamy white cattle which provided the citizens with all the food they needed. A little higher up the valley, mountain streams rushing down between the rocks, sometimes in a tense, plaited silence of dark water, sometimes breaking into noisy white falls, united in a single river, to flow swift but untroubled through the city and the fields below it.

The Cats' houses can best be likened to pagodas, for they were lighter and more intricate than any Gothic spire. It was the custom for each new generation, when it inherited the family dwelling, to carve and paint another tier to be added to the summit of the spire – a practice which had resulted in a curious diversity. Yet the diversity was always harmonious; the slender houses rose from their slopes with the grace and perfect grouping of chestnut blossom on a spreading branch. In their gardens, all of which were private, the Cats grew rare varieties of everlasting-flower, aloes, and the cactuses whose brilliant petals break so unexpectedly from the harsh body of the plant.

The city was enclosed by walls which showed pleasing irregularities of height and direction as they followed the contours of the ground. Because it had become unusual for any Cat to go beyond the walls, many of the gates had fallen into disuse, some being converted into fountains, others into niches for the reception of statues. Only a small wicket on the upper side of the town and a large gatehouse on the lower remained open. The rampart walks, too, once vigilantly patrolled by the city guard, had lapsed wholly into peacefulness. They now offered a delightful promenade where the younger citizens could take the air after dark.

During certain periods of the day, and most universally during the hour before sunset, the Cats would retire into their houses, seat themselves with their tails curled tightly round their paws, and then, by feline concentration, whip themselves into more and more exalted realms of meditation. They sat absolutely motionless, even the tips of their tails poised and still. Only the black pupils of their eyes dilated and contracted again within the tawny circle of the iris.

For many generations now, the purr of these Cats had ceased to make any sound audible to the normal ear, but, as they sat in contemplation, their bodies vibrated with an unseen intensity which caused tremors to run through the delicate fabric of the houses and sound the swarms of little bells hanging on hair-fine threads in every tier of the pagodas. So it was that during the contemplative hours a harmony of exquisite felicity hung like a cloud about the city. Joining with the natural music of the waterfalls it would float up the valley.

It was down the valley that the Dogs had their residential suburb: many rows of comfortable kennels, all with identical gabled roofs and all painted either bottle-green or plum. The life work of the Dogs was to tend the Cats. They looked after their cattle, scavenged their streets and kept their houses clean and in order. The better bred of the young bitches were employed as personal maids to groom the Cats' silken coats and to wash and anoint their idle-tender paws. All these tasks had been done by the Dogs from time beyond memory; they did them submissively enough while in the sight of their masters, but round the kennels there was often the growling and whining of discontent.

Among the Cats, the proportion of kittens was becoming smaller and smaller. Litters of more than two were never born (or if they were, because such grossness would have provoked social ostracism, the totals were discreetly adjusted). Newborn kittens were given small bitches as wet-nurses, and were afterwards segregated in boarding-schools. These schools were staffed by Cats whose faulty powers of vibration barred them from society; either they suffered the embarrassment of an audible purr or their vibrations were too weak, too little concentrated, to produce a true bell harmony. The teachers were so much aware of these shortcomings, however, that no other Cats could have imposed a more exact discipline in training the kittens to develop the powers and accomplishments which they themselves lacked.

Besides these schools the only other public establishment occupied a large house on the outskirts of the city. All the citizens knew of its existence, but they were far too well-bred to make it a subject for conversation; when, occasionally, it had to be mentioned, it was spoken of simply as the Establishment. Here numbers of mice were kept, and young Cats of both sexes. It was an exceedingly well-conducted institution and outwardly decorous.

Although the Cats always ignored the fact, neither they nor their Dog servants could fail to notice how surely the population of the city was declining; dozens of houses stood empty and their spires silent. As a result some of the Dogs were out of work and hung about thinking savagely of the big litters squirming in the corners of the kennels at home. To a sensitive visitor it would have been clear that some long-maintained balance, some delicate adjustment of stresses, was about to be upset.

The hour found its inevitable instrument. A clever mongrel who had forfeited his job as confidential servant to the Chief Conductor of the city worked skilfully upon the general discontent. He exhorted his fellows to take courage and end their servitude to useless, vicious and exacting masters. One evening when the bell music was at its height and the valley full of the ravishing sound, a fearful clamour broke out in the Dogs' suburb, a hideous medley of barks of every pitch. Behind their leader, the Dogs crowded up the valley to attack the city. Perfect order had existed for so long that the Cats had neglected to appoint a single watchman or sentinel. The gates were opened by a master from the Tom-kittens' school, embittered into treachery by a conviction that his purr had been falsely pronounced to be audible.

It was a matter of quick butchery. The Cats, high in their ecstatic contemplation, could not descend to notice a physical danger, and it is doubtful had they done so whether they would have seen fit either to fly or to resist. As it was, the bells of every inhabited pagoda sounded until the very last moment. When the slaughter was over (and in the confusion even the treacherous schoolmaster was not spared) the larger Dogs set to work to destroy all the houses, whose fine appointments they could not enjoy. Soon the river was full of carved spars and painted panels jostling down towards the sea. The thousands of bells, breaking from their hair suspension, sank down and gathered for a moment in lovely shoals along the river bottom. They drifted there as transparent as noon-day moons, grew yet fainter until they resembled the hardly lit burden of a new moon, then disappeared. Silenced already by the water, now they were for ever choked in mud.

The next few days the Dogs spent in dragging up their kennels to the site of the destroyed city – the mongrel taking good care that his went to the place where formerly the Chief Conductor's pagoda had stood. When the work was finished and the Dogs' suburb looked almost exactly the same in its new position as it had done before the move, a tremendous feast was held. Scores of the Cats' milch cows were eaten flesh and bone together, washed down with fermented milk found in the cellars of the Establishment. Afterwards there was a mighty outburst of baying to the moon.

Once the feast was over, the Dogs could find no further source of jubilation. The food was much as before, the kennels were not greatly improved by the tasteless application of Cat paints, and the Dogs could find no change in themselves that was not for the worse. They were suffering from a terrible formlessness and lack of purpose in their new, free lives. A number of the bitches, those who had been lady's-maids or wet-nurses, were frankly heartbroken by the loss of their mistresses or charges, and their emotion soon affected their mates. There was faction and unrest to fill the vacancy of the days; several murders culminated in the disappearance of the mongrel in circumstances which could not be explained until his body was found in the river.

After this a few of the more responsible Dogs formed a Council to debate what should be done. Their meetings were unprofitable because not only were the Councillors quite incapable of understanding what was wrong, but no one of them individually would admit anything was wrong at all. After several Councils had broken up in snappish irritability, a suitable solution was agreed: it consisted in shifting responsibility to a higher authority.

The Dogs knew their former masters had reverenced a mysterious person who lived in a cave beside the small, black mountain lake at the very top of the valley. Ceremonial visits had been regularly paid him by the Cats, for it was he who made the bells on which their music depended. Gathering rock crystal on the mountains he carved it into domes as thin as bubbles, and inside fixed clappers of ground and polished crystals. The clappers hung like bright, petrified tears; the Cats had always believed that the threads which tied them were the Bell-Maker's own hairs. This Bell-Maker possessed a most extraordinary sense of pitch, and there is no doubt that his profession had empowered him to create and control the marvellous harmony of all the city bells in unison.

No Dog had ever before approached his cave, but now a small deputation mounted through the wicket gate and wound up between the rocks. Following a narrow track worn by the Cats, its members were conscious of clumsiness and of the gross size and hairiness of their paws. At last they were led to the cave by a beam of darkness cutting through the sunshine, yet inside they could not detect the source from which it shone; indeed, they could see nothing at all. They called to the Bell-Maker, begging him to show himself and command them what they should do.

No one came, but words seemed to shape themselves in the beam.

'I never appeared in person even to the Cats. I will tell you, as I told them, to imagine me as fulfilling your own ideal conception of yourselves. This saves trouble, for whatever I may say or do, you are certain to make that mistake. What do you want of me?'

'Sire,' they replied, 'we killed the Cats because they were vile parasites upon us Dogs. We thought everything would be much better without them, but it hasn't turned out quite as we expected, and now our lives are both dull and unsafe. We beg you not to blame us for the death of the Cats; we exterminated them because we believed it to be our duty to rid the world of such worthless creatures.'

'Much as I miss the harmony which rose up from the city and brought me the food of rapture, I do not blame you any more than I blame them; the situation was too much for you. I condemn you only for the self-delusion which makes you attempt to disguise your very natural greed and jealousy with talk of duty and high moral purposes. If you will repent this, and also the arrogance you showed in assuming that any change you made in the old order must be for the better, I will do what I can to help you to serve me and yourselves.'

The Dogs all drooped their tails as a mark of their grateful humility, and the Bell-Maker went on:

'First you must impose a severe discipline upon yourselves. Give your life shape by setting limits upon it. You should not eat so much or such coarse food, you should neither bark so loudly and senselessly when you are pleased nor snarl and quarrel at other times. Without weakening them, you must constantly deny and prune your lusts. In such details as your personal habits, you should take scrupulous care of your coats until perhaps you may make them finer and more silky; it would be no bad thing to introduce some artificial fashions such as shaping your ears or docking your tails. You should always be ready to listen to the advice of the bitches and to try to please them, for they will instinctively understand these matters better than you can.

'When you have persevered in such disciplines you may find you are less clumsy and more able to make things of some beauty. You might start by improving the architecture and decoration of your kennels; then, because you are by nature more gregarious than the Cats, you would probably get great satisfaction from noble public buildings. Finally, you must labour to rise to purposes altogether higher. I doubt whether you will ever achieve anything comparable to the harmonies of the Cats, but between us we must try to intensify and shape your instinct for baying at the moon. And don't forget that if you are to do these things really well you will have to find willing servants. Now leave me, and perhaps in a century your descendants may accomplish something.'

The rest of the Dogs shambled down the hill much bewildered by what they had been told, but the most intelligent of them stayed behind to say:

'But, Sire, High Bell-Maker, if we do as you have commanded, shall we not grow very much like the Cats whom we have destroyed?'

'No,' the words slid quietly down the beam, 'not like the Cats; that is your absolute justification. If you are both diligent and fortunate you may perhaps learn to express the essence of your kind. Go and see what you can do, but remember, it is likely enough you will fail altogether. The Cats, after all, were a most remarkable people.'

from *Fables* by Jacquetta Hawkes

For this cat, much thanks

Madam,

I was so perfectly yours before, that I imagin'd you ought to have believ'd there was no need of Presents to secure me to you, nor that you shou'd have contriv'd to catch me like a Rat, with a Cat. However, I must needs own, that your Liberality has created in me some new Affection for you; and if there had yet been anything in my Soul that was stragling from your Service, the Cat you sent me has caught it, and now it is intirely your own. 'Tis certainly the most beautiful and jolliest Cat that e'er was seen: The greatest Beau-cat of Spain, is but a dirty Puss compar'd to him; and Rominagrobis himself, whom you know, Madam, is Prince of the Cats, has no better a Mein, nor can better *smell* out his Interest. I can only say, that 'tis very hard to keep him in, and that of a Cat brought up in Religion, he is the most uneasie to be confin'd to a Cloyster. He can never see a Window open, but immediately he is jumping out of it; he had ere this leap'd twenty times over the Walls, had he not been prevented; and there is no Secular Cat in Christendom that is more a Libertine, or more head-strong than he. I am in hopes, however, that I shall perswade him to stay by the kind Entertainment I give him; for I treat him with nothing but good Cheese and *Naples*–Biskets; and perhaps (Madam) he was not so well treated by you: For I fancy the Ladies of — don't suffer their Cats to go into their Cupboards, and that the austerity of the Convent won't afford 'em such good Chear. He begins to grow tame already; Yesterday I thought verily he had torn off one of my Hands in his wanton Addresses. 'Tis doubtless one of the most playful Creatures in the World; there's neither Man, Woman nor Child, in my Lodging, that wears not some Mark of his Favour. But however lovely he is in his own Person, it shall always be for your sake that I esteem him; and I shall love him so well, for the Love I have for you, that I hope to give occasion to alter the Proverb, and that hereafter it shall be said, *Who Loves me, Loves my Cat*. If besides this Present you will given me the Raven that you promis'd me; and if you will send me the little Dog in a hand-basket one of these Days, you may as proudly say that you have given me all the sorts of Beasts that I love, and every way oblig'd me to be, all the Days of my Life,

Yours, etc.

letter from Vincent Voiture (1598–1648) to a certain Lady-Abbess, translated by William Oldys (1696–1761)

68. Sign carved in wood over the door of 'The Cat and Fiddle', Hinton Admiral, Hampshire

69. *Left:* Sign of the 'Cat and Fiddle', Clyst St Mary, Devon
70. *Right:* Sign of the 'Cat and Fiddle', Bodmin, Cornwall

71. Sign of the 'Mad Cat', Pidley, Huntingdonshire
72. Sign of the 'Squinting Cat', Beckwithshaw, Yorkshire

73. Floor of the porch of the 'Puss in Boots', Macclesfield
74. Sign of the 'Cat and Bagpipes', East Harlsey, Yorkshire

The cat and fiddle

'In the second place, I would forbid that creatures of jarring and incongruous natures should be joined together in the same sign; such as the Bell and the Neat's Tongue, the Dog and the Gridiron. The Fox and the Goose may be supposed to have met, but what have the Fox and the Seven Stars to do together? As for the *Cat and Fiddle*, there is a conceit in it; and therefore I do not intend that anything I have said should affect it.'

So said the writer of a letter published in one of Addison's essays in the *Spectator* in 1710. Lovers of inn-signs and of nursery rhymes will both be glad to know of the *Spectator's* approval of the 'Cat and Fiddle', although, taken literally, cats and fiddles have little in common. It is, as the writer of the letter says, 'a conceit', like that other highly popular inn-sign, the 'Pig and Whistle', and, like the 'Pig and Whistle', has been the subject of much speculation as to origin. None of the solutions are very convincing and most are guesses. The corruption from 'Le Chat Fidèle' is at least plausible, and there is said to have been an inn kept by a Frenchman at Faringdon in Devon, which he called 'A la Chatte Fidèle' after a favourite cat named *Mignonette*. Some attribute the origin to 'Caton le Fidèle', by some accounts a staunch protestant in the reign of Queen Mary, and by others a loyal governor of Calais.

Larwood and Hotten in their work on English inn-signs do not favour this theory for, they say, 'as early as 1587 we find Henry Carr, signe of the Catte and Fidle in the Old Chaunge'; they suggest that this would mean too rapid a corruption of 'Caton le Fidèle'. Yet Mary died in 1558 and thirty years is not too short a period for habitués to have nicknamed the house 'Cat and Fiddle'.

'The only apparent connection between the animal and the instrument', remark the same authors, 'is that the strings are or were made from the cat's entrails.' This is, of course, a complete misconception. Fiddle strings have never been made of cats' guts, which are altogether unsuitable. They were usually made from the intestines of sheep and sometimes of horses or mules. The term 'cat-gut' is sometimes derived from 'gut-cord' but could more plausibly have come from 'kit-gut', 'kit' being the small pocket fiddle which at one time was the instrument much used by dancing masters – as devotees of *Bleak House* and Mr Turveydrop will remember.

One can imagine an innkeeper advertising his house as one where one could hear the 'Kit or Fiddle' and what more likely that customers thinking of 'kit' as 'kitten', should dub the house the 'Cat and Fiddle', whereas 'kit' in this case is probably derived from the Greek κιθαρα, a stringed instrument played with a plectrum.

There being no authentically established explanation of 'Cat and Fiddle', one may give rein to fancy – 'Kit', after all, was a diminutive of Christopher, patron saint of wayfarers, and who more suitable as the patron of an inn frequented by the faithful? Hence, by corruption, to 'Cat and Fiddle'.

Whatever the derivation, there are quite a number of inns of the name. It is said to have been common in Hampshire and one of the best known and most ancient is to be found at Hinton Admiral, on the edge of the New Forest. Here are three representations, all different, one on each side of a swinging sign and one carved in wood over the door. Here, too, we get a further pointer to the origin of the name, for it is stated that the inn was established by the Saxon monastery of Christchurch Twynham in the eleventh century and that the house is in *Domesday Book* as the 'House of Caterine la Fidèle'. The obscurity of this 'Caterine' doubtless led some authorities to claim her without close enquiry as Catherine of Aragon while others have said that the Caterine la fidèle whose name became 'Cat and Fiddle' was Catherine, wife of Peter the Great of Russia. If this inn was indeed founded in the eleventh century, date rules out both Catherine of Aragon and the much more far-fetched Catherine of Russia.

Similar to one of these signs is a very charming one at Clyst St Mary, a few miles out of Exeter on the Sidmouth road. Others are to be found at Bodmin in Cornwall; at Norwich; and on the road across the moors between Buxton in Derbyshire and Macclesfield in Cheshire. The latter, believed to have been established in the eighteenth century, is, at 1690 feet, the highest 'cat' inn in England and is said to be the second highest inn in the country. In this case we get back to 'Caton le Fidèle' as origin. Huguenot silk weavers came to Congleton in the reign of Elizabeth I, under the leadership of a man named Caton and were granted rights on the moorland on which the inn now stands. Shaped stones have been discovered at the boundaries of the concession with the letters C.A.T. F.I.D.E.L. The three hundred years, however, which elapsed between the eighteenth-century inn and the fifteenth-century silk weaver makes the connection at least doubtful. Of this inn it is pleasantly related that a previous Duke of Devonshire, as the owner, used to drive to visit it taking with him a cat and a fiddle.

In Macclesfield there is a 'Puss-in-Boots' and it is a local joke that 'Puss-in-Boots' can never pay a call on the 'Cat and Fiddle' because there is a 'Setter Dog' – another inn – on the road between. There is a second 'Puss-in-Boots' not so far away, at Windley in Derbyshire, and these two are said to commemorate a local highwayman who worked the road between and whose approach was catlike in his silence.

It is odd that several of the 'Cat and Fiddle' signs depict the cat playing a 'cello, the instrument generally being about as large as the performer; and even when the instrument is a genuine fiddle, as in Bodmin, the relationship between the paws, the bow and the violin is extraordinary. This is the more curious when one examines the work of the mediaeval carvers on misericords, so often closely connected with inn-sign art. In these, puss has no difficulty in holding bow and fiddle correctly.

There are, of course, many other cat inn-signs besides the 'Cat and Fiddle', but the only other instrumentalist is to be found at East Harlsey in Yorkshire where a marmalade cat dressed in full Highland regimentals is playing the bagpipes. Here the 'Cat and Bagpipes' is supposed to be a satirical reflection on the Scottish drovers using the Great North Road. It is said that the 'Cat and Bagpipes' as an inn-sign used at one time to be common in Ireland and we are also told that something over a hundred years ago there was a house of that name at the corner of Downing Street where Foreign Office clerks used to lunch.

Like many other inn names and signs, cats appear in various combinations. Some trace descent from religious ideas. Such is the 'Cat and Wheel' in Bristol. There have been several inns of this name and one must turn for an explanation to *Aenigmatical Characters* published in 1665 by Richard Flecknoe, who wrote –

'As for the signs they have pretty well begun their reformation already, changing the sign of the *Salutation* of Our Lady into the *Souldier & Citizen*, and the *Catherine Wheel* into the *Cat and Wheel*; such ridiculous work they make of this reformation and so jealous they are against all mirth and jollity, as they would pluck down *the Cat and Fiddle* too, if it durst but play so loud as they might hear it.'

This passage, of course, referred to the revulsion of the Puritans to anything smelling of Popery. There must be no reference to the Virgin Mary nor yet even to St Catherine and her wheel. Oddly enough, the 'Salutation' was not always changed and Larwood tells us that at one time in London there were four.

One of these was in Newgate Street and this was once called the 'Salutation and Cat', a strange combination of signs and one that could hardly have pleased the correspondent of the *Spectator* quoted at the head of this chapter. The 'Salutation and Cat' counted many well-known eighteenth-century authors among its clients; one of them, Samuel Coleridge, lived in this tavern during one of his periods of melancholia until discovered by Southey who induced him to leave and live a normal life. Here Coleridge used to meet Lamb. They were both Christ's Hospital boys and the school was but a short distance away. After he had left London for the country Coleridge wrote to Lamb:

'When I read in your little volume your nineteenth effusion, or what you call "The Sigh", I think I hear *you* again. I imagine to myself the little smoky room at the *Salutation and Cat*, where we have sat together through the winter nights, beguiling the cares of life with poesy.'

One might well be puzzled by the addition of 'Cat' in the 'Salutation and Cat' but this, according to Brewer, is merely due to the fact that arrangements were made at that particular tavern for the playing of 'Tip-Cat'. A less refined significance is to be found in the vulgar nickname for this tavern – the 'How-de-do-and-spew'. Nicknames play a prominent part in the naming of inns and it is not always easy to find out how and why they occurred. Why should the 'Red Lion' at Paddlesworth in Kent be known as the 'Cat and Custard-pot'? There is, in fact, a 'Cat and Custard-pot' in its own right at Shipton Moyne in Gloucestershire, taken from the inn of that name in Surtees' *Handley Cross*. Cats are not commonly addicted to custard, yet on the Shipton Moyne sign a cat has his head deep in a pot savouring the last mouthful.

The 'Monkey Shaves the Cat' is another odd nickname given to Exeter Railway Tavern, in Bristol. Here there used to be stuffed animals depicting the scene. There is a close ecclesiastical counterpart of this conceit in Beverley Minster, where on the 'supporter' of a misericord a monkey is shown combing a cat.

Quite a number of inns are named with a view to the provender provided. Such are the 'Round of Beef' and the 'Shoulder of Mutton'. In one case the latter became the 'Shoulder of Mutton and Cat'. Larwood quotes a verse which was on the sign of the eighteenth-century inn of that name in Hackney:

> Pray Puss, don't tear,
> For the mutton is so dear;
> Pray Puss, don't claw,
> For the mutton yet is raw.

The sign depicted a thieving cat being chased by a terrier and was supposed by some to be a warning to indifferently honest customers. Later on, the 'Shoulder of Mutton and Cat' was simplified into the 'Cat and Mutton'.

Plain 'Cats' are rare; there are two in Cumberland, one at Egremont and one at Whitehaven but neither has a pictorial sign. There are a few coloured cats, such as the 'Black Cat', one formerly in Lancaster and one near Chesham; a 'Tabby Cat' at West Grinstead in Sussex; a white cat called the 'Charlton Cat' at Charlton in Wiltshire; and a 'Red Cat' in Birkenhead.

Where one finds the domestic cat mixed up with one of the great cats, as in the 'Cat and Lion', at Stockport and at Stretton, Cheshire, Larwood and Hotten suggest that it was originally the 'Tiger and Lion'; this sign, still to be seen at Stretton, has on it the verse:

> The Lion is strong, the Cat is vicious,
> My ale is strong and so is my liquors.

Whether the 'Cat and Tiger' at Sevenoaks should properly be the 'Lion and Tiger', the authorities do not say.

148

Yorkshire is strong in cat inns. Halifax had two, the 'Cat i' th' Wall' and the 'Cat i' th' Window'. They are believed to be named after stuffed pet cats. These won nicknames from the habitués; the nicknames remained and the original names were forgotten. Near Halifax, too, at Wainstalls in a fold in the hills, there is a 'Cat i' th' Well', the origin of the name being unknown, although there is a pleasant sign showing puss in a bucket looking out of the well. Further north, there are two 'Squinting Cats', one of which has a hideously squinting animal on the sign, the inn serving a new housing estate on the outskirts of Leeds. The other, the original 'Squinting Cat', is at Beckwithshaw near Harrogate. The inn has two signs, one being the silhouette of a black cat with glittering, squinting eyes, hanging on the corner of the house and the other a rather charming puss, with a cast, engraved on the window of the bar-parlour.

As one would expect, London used to have a number of taverns named 'Whittington and Cat'. Larwood and Hotten mention, among others, the one on Highgate Hill, which had in its window the skeleton of a cat, which the credulous firmly believed to be the mortal remains of Sir Richard's own puss. (But see 'A cat's a cat', page 27.) The cat is commemorated to this day by a monument on the pavement nearby.

There was said to be an inn in the city of London at one time known as the 'Two Sneezing Cats', but this has proved impossible to trace and it seems more likely to have been the sign of a tobacconist and snuff-seller. Signs were not, of course, by any means confined to inns and taverns, but were affected by most traders in a community which was largely illiterate – though why a bookseller named Thomas Pauer put up a sign over his shop near the Royal Exchange, in 1612, depicting a cat and parrot is hard to explain. A common sign used to be a cat trying to pull a bird out of a cage. This was a derivation of the 'Cat in the Cage', which, in its turn, probably originated with the *Cat in the Basket*. This was a 'live' sign, which decorated drinking booths on the Thames when the river was frozen over in the winter of 1739–40 and consisted of a live cat in a basket. There is a print in Crowle Pennant, vol. VIII, showing such a booth at a later date, with revellers within, the booth described as the *ORIGINAL Cat in the Cage*. The 'cat in the basket' used to be a cruel game in which 'sportsmen' shot at the cat.

Cruelty to cats is also illustrated in two other signs both extant today. One is in the Isle of Grain and shows a cat terrified by an exploding firework, the house being known as the 'Cat and Cracker'. The other is the 'Mad Cat' at Pidley in Huntingdonshire, where there is a finely painted sign of a black cat driven demented by a tin tied to its tail.

Cats appeared on signs abroad as well as in England; there is said to be a French *estaminet* known as 'A La Chatte Qui Pêche' and there was at one time in Lille another called, strangely, 'Aux Chats Bossus', (The Hunchbacked Cats). The French author Fonseca, in *La Haye*, published in 1853, tells of a Frenchman named Bertrand, who retired from France to The

Hague about 1650 to escape the consequences of participation in a conspiracy against Cardinal Mazarin. He set up a cutler's business and over it a sign with a red cat on one side and a portrait of Mazarin in his red robe on the other. Beneath, he had inscribed the legend 'Aux Deux Méchantes Bêtes'. However he altered the sign on the urgent plea of the Burgomaster, who was nervous of French reactions. So Mazarin's face was painted out and another red cat put in the Cardinal's place. Fonseca declared that, even as late as his day, there was a Bertrand at the sign of the 'Red Cat' at The Hague.

There used to be many, and still are quite a number, of animal inn-signs depicting the mother and her litter, such as the 'Sow and Pigs', which is probably the commonest, but so far as can be ascertained there has been only one 'Cat and Kittens', a sign which marked a tavern in Eastcheap in 1823. But a sentimental connotation, of the happy mother cat giving her kittens a drink at their usual tap was only a secondary meaning. In fact the 'cat' and the 'kittens' were the large and small pewter pots in which the ales and spirits were measured out. And on this rather prosaic note we may perhaps leave our tavern cats to their beer.

The convert

As an immature youth I thought nothing could be merrier
Than a wire-haired terrier;
I would pat the nose of an Alsatian
Without trepidation;
I loved dachshunds
That bark with foreign achshunds,
I forgave even Pekinese
For their endless bronchitis, their yapping, their waddle suggesting
    wekinese;
Lugubrious Labradors, sloppy spaniels, ghostly Bedlingtons, even those
    crew-cut corgis,
I loved them all, I loved all dorgis.

My first break with dogs came in Kensington Gardens;
My heart still hardens
When I think of that boxer trying to drown the spaniel
In the Round Pond, and everybody staring, except fool Jennings, who
    rushed in like Solomon or Daniel.
The boxer bit me to the bone, I was a hero,
But people's interest in me was zero,
They clustered round the spaniel (which hadn't fought back at all, that's
    the trouble with dogs, they're either sadistic or yellow),
Saying 'Poor little fellow.'

Then I found that, by any tests,
Dogs are *terrible* as guests;
We look after somebody's dog, and it wanders from room to room, all
    restless and moaning, it doesn't accept us as master and missus;
A dog says ME ME ME, it's just a gauche Narcissus;
But when we leave our cat, she just greets her hostess politely, then goes
    to change for dinner up in the attic.
I've lost my taste for dogs, my taste is aristocratic.

I've heard of police dogs, but I bet they bite the wrong people; I bet
    they're too stupid to be effective.
They only pound the beat; if cats were in the police they'd never come
    below the rank of detective.

If the animals had television,
Dogs would stare at it all day long, but cats can entertain themselves,
  singing madrigals with taste and precision,
And one cat alone'll
Give a fair imitation of a modern violin concerto, all subtle and atonal –
But when a dog barks (as he does too often) he
Sounds like the tearing of giant emery paper, the world's worst
  cacophony. . . .
  But let me not too harshly end,
  I can't quite hate Man's Second Best Friend.

from *Oddly Enough* by Paul Jennings, the *Observer*, 1956

Tobermory

It was a chill, rain-washed afternoon of a late August day, that indefinite season when partridges are still in security or cold storage, and there is nothing to hunt – unless one is bounded on the north by the Bristol Channel, in which case one may lawfully gallop after fat red stags. Lady Blemley's house-party was not bounded on the north by the Bristol Channel, hence there was a full gathering of her guests round the tea-table on this particular afternoon. And, in spite of the blankness of the season and the triteness of the occasion, there was no trace in the company of that fatigued restlessness which means a dread of the pianola and a subdued hankering for auction bridge. The undisguised open-mouthed attention of the entire party was fixed on the homely negative personality of Mr Cornelius Appin. Of all her guests, he was the one who had come to Lady Blemley with the vaguest reputation. Some one had said he was 'clever', and he had got his invitation in the moderate expectation, on the part of his hostess, that some portion at least of his cleverness would be contributed to the general entertainment. Until tea-time that day she had been unable to discover in what direction, if any, his cleverness lay. He was neither a wit nor a croquet champion, a hypnotic force nor a begetter of amateur theatricals. Neither did his exterior suggest the sort of man in whom women are willing to pardon a generous measure of mental deficiency. He had subsided into mere Mr Appin, and the Cornelius seemed a piece of transparent baptismal bluff. And now he was claiming to have launched on the world a discovery beside which the invention of gunpowder, of the printing-press, and of steam locomotion were inconsiderable trifles. Science had made bewildering strides in many directions during recent decades, but this thing seemed to belong to the domain of miracle rather then to scientific achievement.

'And do you really ask us to believe,' Sir Wilfrid was saying, 'that you have discovered a means for instructing animals in the art of human speech, and that dear old Tobermory has proved your first successful pupil?'

'It is a problem at which I have worked for the last seventeen years,' said Mr Appin, 'but only during the last eight or nine months have I been rewarded with glimmerings of success. Of course I have experimented with thousands of animals, but latterly only with cats, those wonderful creatures which have assimilated themselves so marvellously with our civilization while retaining all their highly developed feral instincts. Here and there among cats one comes across an outstanding superior intellect, just as one does among the ruck of human beings, and when I made the acquaintance of Tobermory a week ago I saw at once that I was in contact with a "Beyond-cat" of extraordinary intelligence. I had gone far along the road to success in recent experiments; with Tobermory, as you call him, I have reached the goal.'

Mr Appin concluded his remarkable statement in a voice which he strove to divest of a triumphant inflection. No one said 'Rats', though Clovis's lips moved in a monosyllabic contortion which probably invoked those rodents of disbelief.

'And do you mean to say,' asked Miss Resker, after a slight pause, 'that you have taught Tobermory to say and understand easy sentences of one syllable?'

'My dear Miss Resker,' said the wonder-worker patiently, 'one teaches little children and savages and backward adults in that piecemeal fashion; when one has once solved the problem of making a beginning with an animal of highly developed intelligence one has no need for those halting methods. Tobermory can speak our language with perfect correctness.'

This time Clovis very distinctly said, 'Beyond-rats!' Sir Wilfrid was more polite, but equally sceptical.

'Hadn't we better have the cat in and judge for ourselves?' suggested Lady Blemley.

Sir Wilfrid went in search of the animal, and the company settled themselves down to the languid expectation of witnessing some more or less adroit drawing-room ventriloquism.

In a minute Sir Wilfrid was back in the room, his face white beneath its tan and his eyes dilated with excitement.

'By Gad, it's true!'

His agitation was unmistakably genuine, and his hearers started forward in a thrill of awakened interest.

Collapsing into an armchair he continued breathlessly: 'I found him dozing in the smoking-room, and called out to him to come for his tea. He blinked at me in his usual way, and I said, "Come on, Toby; don't keep us waiting"; and, by Gad! he drawled out in a most horribly natural voice that he'd come when he dashed well pleased! I nearly jumped out of my skin!'

Appin had preached to absolutely incredulous hearers; Sir Wilfrid's statement carried instant conviction. A Babel-like chorus of startled exclamation arose, amid which the scientist sat mutely enjoying the first fruit of his stupendous discovery.

In the midst of the clamour Tobermory entered the room and made his way with velvet tread and studied unconcern across to the group seated round the tea-table.

A sudden hush of awkwardness and constraint fell on the company. Somehow there seemed an element of embarrassment in addressing on equal terms a domestic cat of acknowledged mental ability.

154

'Will you have some milk, Tobermory?' asked Lady Blemley in a rather strained voice.

'I don't mind if I do,' was the response, couched in a tone of even indifference. A shiver of suppressed excitement went through the listeners, and Lady Blemley might be excused for pouring out the saucerful of milk rather unsteadily.

'I'm afraid I've spilt a good deal of it,' she said apologetically.

'After all, it's not my Axminster,' was Tobermory's rejoinder.

Another silence fell on the group, and then Miss Resker, in her best district-visitor manner, asked if the human language had been difficult to learn. Tobermory looked squarely at her for a moment and then fixed his gaze serenely on the middle distance. It was obvious that boring questions lay outside his scheme of life.

'What do you think of human intelligence?' asked Mavis Pellington lamely.

'Of whose intelligence in particular?' asked Tobermory coldly.

'Oh, well, mine for instance,' said Mavis, with a feeble laugh.

'You put me in an embarrassing position,' said Tobermory, whose tone and attitude certainly did not suggest a shred of embarrassment. 'When your inclusion in this house-party was suggested Sir Wilfrid protested that you were the most brainless woman of his acquaintance, and that there was a wide distinction between hospitality and the care of the feeble-minded. Lady Blemley replied that your lack of brain-power was the precise quality which had earned you your invitation, as you were the only person she could think of who might be idiotic enough to buy their old car. You know, the one they call "The Envy of Sisyphus", because it goes quite nicely up-hill if you push it.'

Lady Blemley's protestations would have had greater effect if she had not casually suggested to Mavis only that morning that the car in question would be just the thing for her down at her Devonshire home.

Major Barfield plunged in heavily to effect a diversion.

'How about your carryings-on with the tortoiseshell puss up at the stables, eh?'

The moment he had said it every one realized the blunder.

'One does not usually discuss these matters in public,' said Tobermory frigidly. 'From a slight observation of your ways since you've been in this house I should imagine you'd find it inconvenient if I were to shift the conversation on to your own little affairs.'

The panic which ensued was not confined to the major.

'Would you like to go and see if cook has got your dinner ready?' suggested Lady Blemley hurriedly, affecting to ignore the fact that it wanted at least two hours to Tobermory's dinner-time.

'Thanks,' said Tobermory, 'not quite so soon after my tea. I don't want to die of indigestion.'

'Cats have nine lives, you know,' said Sir Wilfrid heartily.

'Possibly,' answered Tobermory; 'but only one liver.'

'Adelaide!' said Mrs Cornett, 'do you mean to encourage that cat to go out and gossip about us in the servants' hall?'

The panic had indeed become general. A narrow ornamental balustrade ran in front of most of the bedroom windows at the Towers, and it was recalled with dismay that this had formed a favourite promenade for Tobermory at all hours, whence he could watch the pigeons – and heaven knew what else besides. If he intended to become reminiscent in his present outspoken strain the effect would be something more than disconcerting. Mrs Cornett, who spent much time at her toilet table, and whose complexion was reputed to be of a nomadic though punctual disposition, looked as ill at ease as the Major. Miss Scrawen, who wrote fiercely sensuous poetry and led a blameless life, merely displayed irritation; if you are methodical and virtuous in private you don't necessarily want everyone to know it. Bertie van Tahn, who was so depraved at seventeen that he had long ago given up trying to be any worse, turned a dull shade of gardenia white, but he did not commit the error of dashing out of the room like Odo Finsberry, a young gentleman who was understood to be reading for the Church and who was possibly disturbed at the thought of scandals he might hear concerning other people. Clovis had the presence of mind to maintain a composed exterior; privately he was calculating how long it would take to procure a box of fancy mice through the agency of the *Exchange and Mart* as a species of hush-money.

Even in a delicate situation like the present, Agnes Resker could not endure to remain too long in the background.

'Why did I ever come down here?' she asked dramatically.

Tobermory immediately accepted the opening.

'Judging by what you said to Mrs Cornett on the croquet-lawn yesterday, you were out for food. You described the Blemleys as the dullest people to stay with that you knew, but said they were clever enough to employ a first-rate cook; otherwise they'd find it difficult to get anyone to come down a second time.'

'There's not a word of truth in it! I appeal to Mrs Cornett –' exclaimed the discomfited Agnes.

'Mrs Cornett repeated your remark afterwards to Bertie van Tahn,' continued Tobermory, 'and said, "That woman is a regular Hunger Marcher; she'd go anywhere for four square meals a day," and Bertie van Tahn said –'

At this point the chronicle mercifully ceased. Tobermory had caught a glimpse of the big yellow Tom from the Rectory working his way through the shrubbery towards the stable wing. In a flash he had vanished through the open French window.

With the disappearance of his too brilliant pupil Cornelius Appin found himself beset by a hurricane of bitter upbraiding, anxious inquiry, and frightened entreaty. The responsibility for the situation lay with him, and he must prevent matters from becoming worse. Could Tobermory impart his dangerous gift to other cats? was the first question he had to answer. It was possible, he replied, that he might have initiated his intimate friend the stable puss into his new accomplishment, but it was unlikely that his teaching could have taken a wider range as yet.

'Then,' said Mrs Cornett, 'Tobermory may be a valuable cat and a great pet; but I'm sure you'll agree, Adelaide, that both he and the stable cat must be done away with without delay.'

'You don't suppose I've enjoyed the last quarter of an hour, do you?' said Lady Blemley bitterly. 'My husband and I are very fond of Tobermory – at least, we were before this horrible accomplishment was infused into him; but now, of course, the only thing is to have him destroyed as soon as possible.'

'We can put some strychnine in the scraps he always gets at dinnertime,' said Sir Wilfrid, 'and I will go and drown the stable cat myself. The coachman will be very sore at losing his pet, but I'll say a very catching form of mange has broken out in both cats and we're afraid of it spreading to the kennels.'

'But my great discovery!' expostulated Mr Appin; 'after all my years of research and experiment –'

'You can go and experiment on the short-horns at the farm, who are under proper control,' said Mrs Cornett, 'or the elephants at the Zoological Gardens. They're said to be highly intelligent, and they have this recommendation, that they don't come creeping about our bedrooms and under chairs, and so forth.'

An archangel ecstatically proclaiming the Millenium, and then finding that it clashed unpardonably with Henley and would have to be indefinitely postponed, could hardly have felt more crestfallen than Cornelius Appin at the reception of his wonderful achievement. Public opinion, however, was against him – in fact, had the general voice been consulted on the subject it is probable that a strong minority vote would have been in favour of including him in the strychnine diet.

Defective train arrangements and a nervous desire to see matters brought to a finish prevented an immediate dispersal of the party, but dinner that evening was not a social success. Sir Wilfrid had had rather a trying time with the stable cat and subsequently with the coachman. Agnes Resker ostentatiously limited her repast to a morsel of dry toast, which she bit as though it were a personal enemy; while Mavis Pellington maintained a vindictive silence throughout the meal. Lady Blemley kept up a flow of what she hoped was conversation, but her attention was fixed on the doorway. A plateful of carefully dosed fish scraps was in readiness on the sideboard, but sweets and savoury and dessert went their way, and no Tobermory appeared either in the dining-room or kitchen.

The sepulchral dinner was cheerful compared with the subsequent vigil in the smoking-room. Eating and drinking had at least supplied a distraction and cloak to the prevailing embarrassment. Bridge was out of the question in the general tension of nerves and tempers, and after Odo Finsberry had given a lugubrious rendering of 'Melisande in the Wood' to a frigid audience, music was tacitly avoided. At eleven the servants went to bed, announcing that the small window in the pantry had been left open as usual for Tobermory's private use. The guests read steadily through the current batch of magazines, and fell back gradually on the 'Badminton Library' and bound volumes of *Punch*. Lady Blemley made periodic visits to the pantry, returning each time with an expression of listless depression which forestalled questioning.

At two o'clock Clovis broke the dominating silence.

'He won't turn up to-night. He's probably in the local newspaper office at the present moment, dictating the first instalment of his reminiscences. Lady What's-her-name's book won't be in it. It will be the event of the day.'

Having made this contribution to the general cheerfulness, Clovis went to bed. At long intervals the various members of the house-party followed his example.

The servants taking round the early tea made a uniform announcement in reply to a uniform question. Tobermory had not returned.

Breakfast was, if anything, a more unpleasant function than dinner had been, but before its conclusion the situation was relieved. Tobermory's corpse was brought in from the shrubbery, where a gardener had just discovered it. From the bites on his throat and the yellow fur which coated his claws it was evident that he had fallen in unequal combat with the big Tom from the Rectory.

By midday most of the guests had quitted the Towers, and after lunch Lady Blemley had sufficiently recovered her spirits to write an extremely nasty letter to the Rectory about the loss of her valuable pet.

Tobermory had been Appin's one successful pupil, and he was destined to have no successor. A few weeks later an elephant in the Dresden Zoological Garden, which had shown no previous signs of irritability, broke loose and killed an Englishman who had apparently been teasing it. The victim's name was variously reported in the papers as Oppin and Eppelin, but his front name was faithfully rendered Cornelius.

'If he was trying German irregular verbs on the poor beast,' said Clovis, 'he deserved all he got.'

from *The Chronicles of Clovis* by Saki (H. H. Munro)

Puss-in-Boots

The story of Puss-in-Boots is the most famous of all cat tales. It formed the subject of the Eleventh Night in Giovanni Francesco Straparola's *Piacevoli Notti*, a book of fairy-tales and fables collected from many sources. It was translated into French in 1585 and the story, as it is best known in England, comes directly from the version by Charles Perrault of the Académie Française, who published a book of *Contes des Fées*, which included *Le Maître Chat,* or *Le Chat Botté*, in 1696.

In Straparola's version, a clever talking cat manages to secure for his master, one Constantine, a fine castle and the King's heiress. Perrault's cat found himself left by will to the youngest son of a miller, who bequeathed his mill to his eldest son, his donkey to his second son and only his cat to the youngest. The cat, of course, proved to be much the most valuable legacy of the three; through his gift of speech and his cunning, he procured wealth and fortune for his master, whom he dubbed 'Le Marquis de Carabas'. It is a pleasant speculation to consider whether the Miller had an inkling of the value of his cat-legacy. The theme of the youngest son coming out best in the end is a favourite one in many fairy tales and one wonders whether the notion was not to suggest that there was unfairness in the theory and practice of primogeniture.

Andrew Lang suggests that the story must have first emerged in an advanced and sophisticated civilization, since the differences between the poor labourers and the rich nobles are so extreme. However this may be, the tale, or its equivalent, is to be found in many countries, there being versions in Scandinavia, Bulgaria, Russia, Finland, Africa, India and elsewhere. The cat of the story is often another animal, as, for instance, in Sicily, where the clever beast is a fox. In this account, the human beneficiary is ungrateful and kills the fox, the moral being to point to man's natural ingratitude. In an Indian version the place of the cat is taken by a match-making jackal, while in Swahili there is a gazelle-in-boots.

The killing of the fox in the Sicilian version suggests that the storyteller found it hard to adduce a satisfactory moral in the normal ending, where the cat and his master live happily ever after. George Cruickshank, who published and illustrated the story in his *Fairy Library*, so objected to the immorality of the tale, which showed cunning and deceit to be successful, that he changed the facts, making out that the hero was in reality the true heir, kept out of his own by the wicked ogre. The cat, he tells us, was the Marquis's gamekeeper, who had been turned into a cat for his evil propensities!

Many of the fables which were favourites in the Europe of the Middle-Ages derived from the *Fables of Bidpai*, the Arabic version of a lost original of the *Panchatantra*, a collection of fables in Sanskrit. It is, of course, impossible to trace the first appearance of the 'puss-in-boots' story, but it may well have been among the fairy tales, myths and legends handed down by word of mouth by primitive storytellers. In its earliest forms, the story recounted, doubtless, the faithfulness of some animal to its master, witness the cat of Ch'en Hai-sang (q.v., page 102), and the embellishment of the boots was probably added in mediaeval times, when writers, artists and carvers delighted in portraying a topsy-turvy world where animals dressed up as human beings, preached, danced, performed on musical instruments and the like. That top-boots can have been anything other than hampering to a cat, of all animals, does not appear to have occurred to the tellers of the tale, although Perrault does suggest that when Puss fled on to the roof at the sight of the ogre in the form of a lion, he found the boots something of a handicap in scampering on the tiles.

Incidents of the story have occurred in other contexts, as when Hesiod tells of Zeus persuading his wife to become a fly and then eating her. One feels that the Ogre knew little of cat-psychology, when he allowed Puss to persuade him to assume the form of a mouse – but then ogres are ogres and notoriously dim-witted, while talking cats are talking cats and a law unto themselves.

There have been many illustrated versions of Puss-in-Boots. Among some of the most striking illustrations are those by Otto Speckter in *Das Märchen vom Gestiefelten Kater,* compiled from the works of Straparola, Perrault and others in 1843. Later Gustave Doré produced some splendid Puss-in-Boots drawings.

As for the story itself, Charles Perrault gives it in its simplest and most effective form. His title, *'Le Maître Chat'*, *ou 'Le Chat Botté'*, is immediately arresting. In English, the second part of the title alone is used, suggesting, perhaps, that in England boots are more than brains. It remained for 'Saki', perhaps unwittingly, to find *le mot juste* for *'Maître'*, when he described the cat Tobermory in his story of that name, as a 'Beyond-Cat'. Puss-in-Boots was certainly a 'beyond-cat'.

The Beyond-Cat or Puss-in-Boots

Translated from the French of Charles Perrault

There was once a miller whose only possessions to leave his three sons were his mill, his donkey and his Cat. The division of the property was soon made and neither notary nor attorney was called in; they would very soon have swallowed up the whole of the poor patrimony. The eldest son

Puss-in-Boots, by George Cruikshank

got the mill, the second the ass, while the youngest had to be content with only the Cat. His disappointment at so wretched a legacy was extreme.

'If my two brothers go into partnership,' said he to himself, 'they'll manage to make an honest living, whereas, when I've eaten my cat and made myself a muff of its skin, there'll be nothing left for me but to die of starvation.'

The Cat, who heard these dreadful words (but pretended not to) said to the young man:

'Not to worry, sir; you've only to give me a bag and get a pair of boots made for me, so that I can get about in the scrub, to see that your portion isn't as bad as you think.'

Although his master set no great store by this assurance, he had seen the Cat play so many clever tricks to catch rats and mice, as when he hung by his feet from a shelf or hid in the meal, pretending to be dead, that he hoped something might come of the Cat's words to help him.

As soon as the Cat had got what he had asked for, he put on his boots boldly, and hung the bag round his neck. Taking the strings of the bag in his fore-paws, he went off to a warren where there were a great many rabbits. Having put some bran and some sow-thistles into his bag, he lay down pretending to be dead and waited for some young rabbit, unversed in the ways of this wicked world, to burrow into the bag to eat whatever was inside it. Hardly had he lain down than he was thrilled to see a scatter-brained young rabbit go into the bag. Instantly the 'beyond'-cat pulled the strings tight, caught the rabbit and killed it without a qualm. He was very proud of his catch and went off with it to pray for an audience of the King. He was shewn into His Majesty's apartments. Bowing low, he said to the King:

'Sire, my master the Marquess of Carabas' (for such was the name by which he had made up his mind to refer to his master), 'has bid me present to your Majesty this rabbit from his warren.'

'Please thank your master for me,' said the King, 'and tell him just how delighted I am with his gift.'

Another day the Cat went and hid himself in a cornfield and when two partridges ventured into his open bag he pulled the strings and caught them both. These, too, he presented to the King, who again expressed pleasure and tipped him handsomely. For two or three months the Cat continued from time to time to take the King gifts of game, the result, he said, of his master's skill in hunting.

One day the Cat heard that the King was going to take a drive by the banks of the river with his daughter, the loveliest of princesses, so he said to his master:

'If you do exactly as I tell you, your fortune's made. All you have to do is to bathe in the river where I tell you and leave the rest to me.'

The Marquess of Carabas did what his Cat told him without the re-motest idea what good it would do him. While he was in the water the King happened to pass and the Cat started to bawl out, 'Help! Help!', at the top of his voice. 'The Marquess of Carabas is drowning!'

Hearing the hullabaloo, the King put his head out of the carriage window. He recognized the Cat who had so often brought him game, and at once commanded his guards to hurry to the assistance of the drowning man. While they were pulling the Marquess out of the river, the Cat told the King that while the Marquess was bathing, thieves had come along and stolen his clothes and run away with them, in spite of the Cat's own shouts of 'Stop Thief!', at the top of his voice. In fact, the funny fellow had himself hidden the clothes behind a big stone.

The King at once told his Gentlemen of the Wardrobe to go and fetch one of his best suits for the Marquess of Carabas. The King paid him a thousand little attentions and as the fine clothes which the Marquess had been given set off his appearance (he was handsome and well-made), the King's daughter found him not a little to her liking; and no sooner had the Marquess glanced at her very respectfully two or three times, than she fell madly in love with him.

The King asked him to join them in the carriage for the rest of the drive. The success of his scheme so thrilled the Cat that he raced on ahead in front of the carriage. When he came upon some labourers mowing a meadow, he said to them:

'Hi! You! If you don't tell the King, when he asks, that this meadow you're mowing belongs to the Marquess of Carabas, I'll make mince-meat of the lot of you!'

When the King came along, he naturally asked the folk whose meadow it was that they were mowing.

'It belongs to the Marquess of Carabas,' they said in chorus, for the Cat's threats had terrified them.

'You've got a jolly nice little property there,' said the King to the Marquess.

'Yes, Sire,' replied the Marquess, 'it's a field which crops very well every year.'

The 'beyond' Cat, who kept on ahead, came on some reapers and said:

'You chaps who are reaping, if you don't tell the King when he questions you, that all this corn belongs to the Marquess of Carabas, I'll make mince-meat of the lot of you!'

Once more, as the King passed and asked to whom all the corn belonged, he was told by the reapers with one voice, 'The Marquess of Carabas!'.

Once more, he congratulated the Marquess.

Still rushing on ahead, the Cat made everyone he met promise to tell the same story, or else! And so the King was amazed at the Marquess's vast wealth.

At last the Cat arrived at a splendid castle which belonged to an ogre, who was quite the richest ogre ever known, for all the countryside through which the King had passed belonged to him and his retainers. The Cat, having taken care to find out what sort of a chap the ogre was and whether he had any wits, called on him and said that he could not think of passing so close to the castle without having the honour of paying his respects.

The Ogre welcomed him as affably as possible, for an ogre, and begged him to stay and rest a little.

'Is it true as I've been told,' said the Cat, 'that you have the magical power of assuming the shape of any animal you fancy and that you can, for instance, become a lion or even an elephant?'

'Absolutely true!' said the Ogre in an off-hand manner. 'Just watch me become a lion.'

When the Cat suddenly saw a lion before him, he was so terrified that he leapt for the eaves, where he was in some danger of falling because of his boots, which were not much good for walking on the tiles. As soon as he saw that the Ogre had resumed his ordinary shape, the Cat came down and admitted that he had been dreadfully frightened.

'Another thing told me,' he said, 'but, you know, I simply can't believe it, is that you can change yourself into one of the smallest animals – a rat, say, or even a mouse. I must say I'm sure such a thing utterly impossible.'

'Impossible my foot!' said the Ogre. 'Just watch me!'

And in less time than it takes to tell, he had become a mouse and run along the floor. No sooner had the Cat seen the mouse than he pounced on it and ate it up.

In the meantime, the King, as he passed, observed the castle and expressed a desire to enter it. The Cat, who heard the noise of the carriage as it crossed the drawbridge, rushed out and said to the King:

'Your Majesty is most welcome to the castle of the Marquess of Carabas!'

'Gracious, my dear Marquess, is this yours too?' exclaimed the King. 'Why, there can be nothing finer than this courtyard and the buildings which surround it. Do let us go in!'

The Marquess gave his hand to the young princess and following the King, who preceded them, they came into a great hall where they found a splendid feast set out. This the Ogre had had prepared as he was expecting friends to dine that very day, but they dared not come when they heard that the King was there.

The King was as greatly taken with the charming manners of the Marquess as the princess, and she was quite crazy about them. Nor had the King failed to be impressed by the Marquess's great possessions. So, having drunk his sixth bumper of wine, he said:

'It only remains for you, my dear Marquess, to decide whether to become my son-in-law. The matter is entirely up to you.'

The Marquess of Carabas made a deep bow and accepted the honour which the King had offered him. That very day he married the princess.

As for the Cat, he became a great personage at Court and never again bothered to chase rats or mice except for amusement.

The nursery cat

So many cats have poured through the nursery that their name is Legion. From the mediaeval paragon, Puss-in-Boots, unnamed save for his famous *soubriquet*, down to that latest master-cat, Orlando, cats have always thrilled the inhabitants of the nursery. Strange, when one thinks of the adult sophistication, which is the prerogative of all cats. Dogs, perhaps, appeal more to the brash teenager, but the cat's wisdom tells him how to win the hearts of children; with them, he understands that make-believe is in truth reality.

It must have been a teenager who had lost the wisdom of the nursery and who had not yet attained to grown-up appreciation of life, that sang that egregious ditty:

> Daddy wouldn't give me a Bow-wow, Bow-wow,
> I've got a little cat
> And I'm very fond of that,
> But I'd rather have a Bow-wow-wow!

'Daddy,' of course understood feline superiority.

And so, dogs are scarce in nursery mythology, while cats innumerable have purred their furry way into the hearts of countless children – and not only children of tender years.

Strangely, the most famous nursery cats are nameless – or have no more than a '*nom-de-guerre*' like Puss-in-Boots. We are never told the name, whether forename or surname, of the celebrated cat who wedded the owl. Nor do we know the appellation of that sinister humorist, the Cheshire Cat. Apart from Puss-in-Boots, of all nursery cats the Cheshire Cat reigns supreme. His is an enigmatic character, possessed of a profound philosophy. Sardonic, but not unkindly, mysterious, but not uninformative, he both captivates and puzzles Alice, who is, perhaps one may say, the apotheosis of all nursery heroines.

Of course, all those cats – and, indeed, other creatures – who have become members of our permanent nursery hierarchy, have won their place in it by capturing the hearts and minds of grown-ups as well as of children. It is related of Lewis Carroll that the idea of the Cheshire Cat came to him while sitting in church at Pot Shrigley, where there is a grotesque cat's face looking out from one of the pillars. The face has little of the charm of the creation which it inspired, yet it is enigmatic; and certainly as it passed through the crucible of Lewis Carroll's mind, it bestowed that quality in a form acceptable to children on the Cheshire Cat. Who can ever forget the ecstasy of contemplating, with Alice, that disappearing grin?

To 'grin like a Cheshire cat' is, however, older than Lewis Carroll. John Bellenden Ker (whose explanation is referred to later in this chapter), wrote of it in 1837, but it has proved impossible to find any satisfactory explanation of the allusion. Cheshire cheeses were at one time moulded in the shape of a cat and this may have had something to do with it. Another suggestion is that it derives from indifferent sign-painters' versions of the Lion Rampant, said to be a common inn-sign in Cheshire. Yet there are plenty of Lions Rampant, in various colours, in many other counties. Its true origin remains a mystery.

The Pussy-cat of *The Owl and the Pussy-cat* is perhaps a more endearing character. While biologists, no doubt, find it a peculiar freak that a cat should mate with an owl, to the nursery it is entirely natural. Owls and cats have a very similar appearance. They both can see in the dark. Above all, they both catch mice. Here is the very essence of nursery philosophy, where reality and fantasy combine on equal terms to create a land of delights, peopled with creatures made to be loved and laughed at with eternal affection. One could not think of leaving out this most charming, complete and concise nursery lyric:

The Owl and the Pussy-cat

The Owl and the Pussy-cat went to sea
   In a beautiful pea-green boat,
They took some honey, and plenty of money,
Wrapped up in a five-pound note.
The Owl looked up to the stars above,
   And sang to a small guitar,
'O lovely Pussy! O Pussy, my love,
   What a beautiful Pussy you are,
         You are,
         You are!
What a beautiful Pussy you are!'

Pussy said to the Owl, 'You elegant fowl!
   How charmingly sweet you sing!
O let us be married! too long we have tarried:
   But what shall we do for a ring?'
They sailed away for a year and a day,
   To the land where the Bong-tree grows,

And there in a wood a Piggy-wig stood
  With a ring at the end of his nose,
      His nose,
      His nose,
  With a ring at the end of his nose.

'Dear Pig, are you willing to sell for one shilling
  Your ring?' Said the Piggy, 'I will.'
So they took it away, and were married next day
By the Turkey who lives on the hill.
They dined on mince, and slices of quince,
  Which they ate with a runcible spoon;
And hand in hand, on the edge of the sand,
  They danced by the light of the moon,
      The moon,
      The moon,
  They danced by the light of the moon.

It is as difficult to analyse the qualities which make good nursery art as those which make good serious art. Incongruity, the unexpected, repetition, – particularly repetition – all go to make up the good nursery story, poem, or picture.

With Edward Lear and Lewis Carroll as creators of supreme nursery cats must be coupled Beatrix Potter, although her cats are, if one may be forgiven the word, in a very different category. They are 'domestic' cats, with the ordinary qualities of the villagers among whom they live. Their adventures are not like those of Lear's Seven Young Cats, who found and chased (until they died of exhaustion) a Clangle-Wangle, against which they had been particularly warned by the Two Old Cats, their parents. Beatrix Potter's cats are cosy people with cosy ordinary lives – indeed, they might well be ordinary villagers and it is by the merest chance that they happen to be cats.

The creator of Orlando and Grace, Kathleen Hale, is a literary offspring of Beatrix Potter and her cats do all the things we do. Her drawings and wit are quite superb, but, unlike Beatrix Potter, Kathleen Hale is not quite consistent in the accounts of the adventures of Orlando and his family. They occasionally stray into the realms of grown-up-ness, as when, on the occasion of Orlando and Grace going dancing, the band plays 'God Save Our Gracious Cat' – a delicious touch, irresistible to grown-ups, but a little beyond the scope of young children – not, in fact, quite 'Potterism'.

What of *The Cat That Walked By Himself*? That consummate craftsman, Rudyard Kipling, in his account of how Cat won his position with mankind, has created a Cat as we all know him. Kipling admits him grudgingly to Society, concedes his charm for young children – but doesn't like him. One suspects him of being one of the 'three proper men out of five' who will always throw things at a cat when they meet him. To Kipling, '. . . when the moon gets up and night comes, he is the Cat that walks by himself, and all places are alike to him. Then he goes out to the Wet Wild Woods, or up the Wet Wild Trees, or on the Wet Wild Roofs, waving his wild tail and walking by his wild lone.'

Must one include Dick Whittington's Cat among nursery cats? Probably not. Little or nothing is known about him. It was the bells, not the cat, that persuaded Dick to go back to London. Besides, if we are to believe some pundits, Sir Richard Whittington's Cat was a boat in which he imported coals from Newcastle to London and not a cat at all! We can, perhaps, leave Dick Whittington and his Cat to Pantomimes, which, as everyone knows, are designed for Women's Institutes and Darby and Joan Clubs, not for the denizens of the nursery.

These, or at any rate the younger ones, generally find the cats which jingle their way through nursery rhymes more to their taste. Oddly enough, the Cat of *Hey diddle diddle* is not much thought of. One at least of the present writers found the athletic cow a more interesting

75. The Cats' Party by Louis Wain (p. 33)

76. Cat Musicians; early 19th century child's picturebook

77. *Der gestiefelte Kater*; title page by Otto Speckter

78. *Above right:* Puss being measured for boots, by Otto Speckter
79. *Below right:* Puss in Boots by Gustave Doré

After dinner they went to the Skating Rink where the orchestra recognised Orlando, and played "God Save Our Gracious Cat."

Tingling all over and with sparkling eyes and frosted whiskers the elegant cats skated divinely to the tune of a waltz.

80. Orlando and Grace skating by Kathleen Hale

81. From *Old Possum's Book of Practical Cats* by T. S. Eliot; drawing by Nicolas Bentley

character and the Dish running away with the Spoon more intriguing than either the fiddle-playing Cat or the Little Dog which laughed.

The rhyme itself is ancient as nursery rhymes go and took a number of forms. John Orchard Halliwell gives it thus:

Hey diddle diddle
The cat and the fiddle
The cow jumped over the moon
The little dog laughed
To see such craft
While the dish ran after the spoon.

He alleges that the rhyme was alluded to in a Tragedy of the sixteenth century, known as *King Cambyses*, but the Opies (authors of the *Oxford Dictionary of Nursery Rhymes*) say that one of the few authenticated statements that can be made about it is that it appeared in print in 1765.

Halliwell, who published *The Nursery Rhymes of England* first in 1842, suggests a Greek derivation in a verse beginning 'Αδ ἀδηλα, δηλα δ'ἀδε, but he omits this in his 1853 edition, which, as the Opies say, looks as if he realized it was a hoax. He does, however, quote a rather pleasant Latin version:

Hei didulum! atque iterum didulum! Felisque fidesque
 Vacca super lunae cornua prosiluit;
Nescio qua catulus risit dulcedine ludi;
 Abstulit et turpi lanx cochleare fuga.

(Here *catulus* is used in the sense of 'puppy'. According to some, it was used by Phaedrus to mean a young cat. *Lanx* is used by both Cicero and Vergil in the sense of a 'plate', while *cochleare* is a 'spoon'; the original meaning of this word is 'something pertaining to snails' and hence it came to mean the spoon or implement with which one removed a snail from its shell.)

Halliwell (who later changed his name to Halliwell-Phillips) was scholar and librarian of Jesus College, Cambridge, and was a noted Shakespearean scholar. Commonsense doubtless saved him from subscribing to the extraordinary theories as to the origin of *Hey diddle diddle* and many other nursery rhymes put forward by John Bellenden Ker (formerly Gawler), who in 1832 published *An Essay on the Archaeology of Popular English Phrases and Nursery Rhymes*. The Opies describe this volume as 'probably the most extraordinary example of misdirected labour in the history of English letters'. Ker sets out to show that many English phrases and nursery rhymes are derived from an early form of Dutch. The Opies declare that Ker invented this curious language himself. Ker's version of *Hey diddle diddle* runs:

Hye! died t'el, died t'el
De quit end de vied t'el.
De kauw j'hunnt; 'Hoever cet; dij moê aen.'
De lij t'el dogue laft tot sij sus sport
Hon yi te dies; 'Rar! haft er dij spaê oen.'

Interpreted by Ker himself, this gibberish is supposed to mean:

'You that work hard for your bread, do contrive among yourselves to shame the common thief and mischiefmaker. This Jackdaw (priest) keeps on repeating "Plough the land duly; be painstaking, my man!" And this curse to every virtue continues harping on the same strain until he is stopped short. Be sure you salute him at once with, "My active fellow, take you this spade and get your own bread with it honestly, and don't filch from others".'

It would be tedious to detail much of John Bellenden Ker's extravaganza. He even has an explanation for 'He grinned like a Cheshire Cat', in his pet Old Dutch: 'Hij geur i'nnt lijcker j'hesse, schier kaet.' This strange rigmarole, he declares, means, 'He produces an unpleasant effect in the place he comes into, like some he-cat, whose presence is only perceived by the smell it brings in with it.'

Usually the cat's instrument in rhyme, on carvings or in mediaeval manuscripts is the fiddle, although very occasionally he is playing the bagpipes. It is unusual to have both instruments together as in the rhyme:

A cat came fiddling out of a barn
With a pair of bagpipes under her arm;
She could sing nothing but 'fiddle-cum-fee,
The mouse has married the humble-bee.'
Pipe, cat; dance, mouse;
We'll have a wedding at our good house.

A version not unlike this appeared in a Wiltshire manuscript of 1740 and so far as is known, this, according to the Opies, is the earliest. But the fact of the fiddle being puss's pet instrument is supported by another rhyme quoted by Halliwell:

Come, dance a jig
To my granny's pig,
With a rowdy dowdy dowdy;
Come, dance a jig
To my granny's pig
And pussy-cat shall crowdy.

'Crowdy' means to play the crwth, a very early member of the fiddle family and suggests the antiquity of the rhyme. Nursery rhymes do not, however, as a rule, have a very ancient lineage, the early nineteenth century being the most usual period for their first appearance in print, though some, of course, are earlier. Halliwell quotes, in 1853:

> Diddlety, diddlety, dumpty,
> The cat ran up the plum-tree;
> Half-a-crown to fetch her down!
> Diddlety, diddlety, dumpty.

For some reason, say the Opies, cats in song frequently take refuge in plum trees, and they mention:

'Lady come down and see the Cat sits in the Plum-tree', which is to be found as early as 1609, in *Pammelia, Musick's Miscellanie*.

Ding dong, Bell appears to have an even earlier origin and is said to have been 'collected' by one John Lant, an organist of Winchester Cathedral, in 1580. His version, also in *Pammelia*, runs:

> Jacke boy, ho boy, newes,
> The cat is in the well,
> Let us ring now for her knell,
> Ding dong, Ding dong, Bell.

There are, of course, many pleasant rhymes both ancient and modern about cats, far too many to quote. One which may not be familiar south of the Border is:

> Dingle dingle-dousie;
> The cat's a' lousy;
> Dingle dingle-dousie,
> The dog's a' fleas;
> Dingle dingle-dousie,
> Be crouse ay, be crouse ay;
> Dingle dingle-dousie,
> Ye'se hae a brose o' pease.

In J. Mactaggart's *Gallovidian Encyclopaedia*, a 'dingle-dousie' is described as a piece of wood burning red at one end, which a mother would whirl round and round to amuse the children while singing this rhyme.

Some rhymes have doubtless inspired later nursery tales, as, for instance, in the story of *The Tailor of Gloucester*, one of Beatrix Potter's most loved stories where the Cat offers to help in the tailoring, exactly as in the rhyme, quoted by Halliwell:

> Some little mice got in a barn to spin;
> Pussy came by and she popped her head in;
> 'Shall I come in and cut your threads off?'
> 'Oh, no, kind Sir, you will snap our heads off!'

One of the few cat nursery rhymes which can unhesitatingly be attributed to a definite author is the verse in *Nursery Nonsense and Rhymes
Without Reason*, written by D'Arcy Wentworth Thompson, one time
classical master at the Edinburgh Academy (and teacher of, among others,
Robert Louis Stevenson and Andrew Lang), for his son, an even more
famous D'Arcy Wentworth Thompson:

> Who's that ringing at my door-bell?
> I'm a little pussy-cat and I'm not very well.
> Then rub your little nose with a little mutton-fat,
> And that's the best thing for a sick pussy-cat.

The verse, like the rest of the book, is charmingly illustrated by C. A.
Bennett.

Probably the most popular of all nursery rhymes about cats is:

> Pussy-cat, Pussy-cat, where have you been?
> I've been up to London to look at the Queen.
> Pussy-cat, Pussy-cat, what did you there?
> I frightened a little mouse under her chair.

Some have said the rhyme referred to Queen Elizabeth but in the *National
Review*, in 1941, Lady Maxse refers to it as a satirical reflection on the
democratic parties given by Queen Caroline.

Chambers Journal in 1842 and later in 1870, has a pleasant Scottish
version:

> Poussie, poussie, baudrons,
> Where hae ye been?
> I've been at London
> Seein' the Queen.
> Poussie, poussie, baudrons,
> What got ye there?
> I got a guid fat mousikie
> Rinnin' up a stair.
> Poussie, poussie, baudrons,
> What did ye do wi't?
> I put it in my meal-pock
> To eat it to my bread.

A charming pair of nursery cats, hardly remembered today, are Minz
and Maunz, the two cats in *Struwwelpeter*, who warned Harriet not to play
with matches and mourned her with deluges of tears when she had
become a little heap of ashes as a result of disregarding their advice.

In writing of nursery cats, too many cry out – perhaps one might say 'miaow' – for mention: the three little kittens who lost their mittens and in less remote times, Felix, the cat 'who went on walking', but perhaps we may let one of the giants of the past have the last word:

"Well, then," the Cat went on, "you see a dog growls when it's angry, and wags its tail when it's pleased. Now *I* growl when I'm pleased, and wag my tail when I'm angry. Therefore I'm mad."

"*I* call it purring, not growling," said Alice.

"Call it what you like," said the Cat. "Do you play croquet with the Queen to-day?"

Some ships' cats

The first ship's cat

Two sorts of animal, however, left the ark without having entered it. They were the pig and the cat. God had created these animals in the ark for a special purpose. The vessel was becoming full of filth and human excrements and the stench was such that it could no longer be endured. When the inmates went and complained to Noah, he passed his hand down the back of the elephant and the pig issued forth and ate up all the filth that was in the ark. Thereupon the inhabitants of the ark once more came to Noah and complained against the rats who were busy in the ark and caused great nuisance. They ate up all the food and plagued the travellers in many other ways. Noah thereupon passed his hand down the back of the lion. The King of the beasts sneezed and a cat leapt out of its nose. The cat at once ate all the rats and the travellers had peace.

from *Myth and Legend of Ancient Israel* by Angelo S. Rappoport

The cat of the Fila Cavena

It chanced by fortune that the shippes Cat lept into the sea, which being downe, kept her selfe very valiauntly above water, notwithstanding the great waves, still swimming, the which the master knowing, he caused the Skiffe with halfe a dozen men to goe towards her and fetch her againe, when she was almost halfe a mile from the shippe, and all this while the shippe lay on staies. I hardly believe they would have made such haste and meanes if one of the company had bene in the like perill. They made the more haste because it was the patrons cat. This I have written onely to note the estimation that cats are in, among the Italians, for generally they esteeme their cattes, as in England we esteeme a good Spaniell. The same night about tenne of the clocke the winde calmed, and because none of the shippe knewe where we were, we let fall an anker about 6 mile from the place we were at before, and there wee had muddie ground at twelve fathome.

from Captain John Locke's account of a voyage from Venice to Jerusalem (from *The Principal Navigations Voyages Traffiques and Discoveries of the English Nation* by Richard Hakluyt, 1589)

Saved by the boatswain

Thursday, July 11th, 1754. A most tragical incident fell out this day at sea. While the ship was under sail, but making as will appear no great way, a kitten, one of four of the feline inhabitants of the cabin, fell from the window into the water: an alarm was immediately given to the captain, who was then upon deck, and received it with the utmost concern and many bitter oaths. He immediately gave orders to the steersman in favour of the poor thing, as he called it; the sails were instantly slackened, and all hands, as the phrase is, employed to recover the poor animal. I was, I own, extremely surprised at all this; less indeed at the captain's extreme tenderness than at his conceiving any possibility of success; for if puss had had nine thousand instead of nine lives, I concluded they had been all lost. The boatswain, however, had more sanguine hopes, for having stripped himself of his jacket, breeches and shirt, he leaped boldly into the water, and to my great astonishment, in a few minutes returned to the ship, bearing the motionless animal in his mouth. Nor was this, I observed, a matter of such great difficulty as it appeared to my ignorance, and possibly may seem to that of my fresh-water reader. The kitten was now exposed to air and sun on the deck, where its life, of which it retained no symptoms, was despaired of by all.

But as I have, perhaps, a little too wantonly endeavoured to raise the tender passions of my readers in this narrative, I should think myself unpardonable if I concluded it without giving them the satisfaction of hearing that the kitten at last recovered, to the great joy of the good captain, but to the great disappointment of some of the sailors, who asserted that the drowning cat was the very surest way of raising a favourable wind; a supposition of which, though we have heard several plausible accounts, we will not presume to assign the true original reason.

from *A Voyage to Lisbon* by Henry Fielding

The cat of the Maria Teresa

In the Spanish-American War of 1898, the Spanish Fleet under Admiral Cervera was blockaded in Santiago harbour, in Cuba, by the American Fleet. The passage from the open sea into the harbour is very narrow and on 3 July 1898, Richmond Pearson Hobson, an American Naval Constructor, with seven volunteers, took the collier S.S. *Merrimac*, intending to sink her in the narrows and thus completely seal up the harbour – actually she was sunk nearly a mile from the narrowest part of the channel.

The exploit, however, had the effect of making it impossible for the Spanish ships to escape by night. Cervera tried to take his ships out while the U.S. crews were at Sunday service. In the resulting battle the whole Spanish Fleet was destroyed. The flagship *Maria Teresa* was driven ashore in flames and Cervera became a prisoner, having left his cat on board. Hobson was made an Admiral for his courage and resource – but what happened to the cat of the *Maria Teresa*?

The ballad of the cat of the Maria Teresa

The Spanish High Admiral put out to sea
In the Flagship *Maria Teresa*,
And I was the cat that went just for the spree.
The ship wore the flag of Commander-in-C,
But I was permitted my private burgee,
For I am an Admiral's cat, don't you see,
The Flag-Cat, *Maria Teresa*.

But alas and alack, we should have put back
In the Flagship *Maria Teresa*.
We hadn't the room in the channel to tack,
Hemmed in as we were by *S.S. Merrimac*.
We could not stand up to the Yankee attack:
Our ship drove ashore and became bric-à-brac
And the wreck of *Maria Teresa*.

The crew and the officers all swam ashore
From the Flagship *Maria Teresa*.
They'd done what they could; indeed, what could they more?
(They might, it is true, have made me Commodore,
But the Admiral said that that wouldn't be war,)
So I stayed with the ship and hid in the store,
As Flag-Cat, *Maria Teresa*.

Cervera, the Admiral, naught if not brave,
In the flagship *Maria Teresa*,
Would have had, if allowed, a watery grave
For failure his master's dominions to save.
To Hobson, who'd won, he said, 'One boon I crave;
Look after my cat, who has had a near shave.
He's the Flag-Cat, *Maria Teresa*.'

Then Admiral Hobson, who had a kind heart,
Said, 'I'll salvage *Maria Teresa*!'

He left me in charge of the ship; this was smart
Because as you'll hear, we'd have been in the cart,
Had I not been familiar with every chart,
From the Horn to the Cape and from Breton to Start,
As Flag-Cat, *Maria Teresa*.

Dear Hobson then made a most dreadful mistake
With the hulk of *Maria Teresa*.
He ordered the *Vulcan*, repair ship, to take
Maria Teresa in tow in her wake
And sail around Cuba to Charleston, to break
Up the ship; he forgot (he was hardly awake)
The Flag-Cat, *Maria Teresa*.

The skipper of *Vulcan*, mean-spirited soul,
Hated *Maria Teresa*.
We met a tornado, got out of control,
The fellow was certain we'd never reach goal,
So severed the tow-rope and left us to roll.
When anchored in Charleston, he had the bells toll
For the Flag-Cat, *Maria Teresa*.

'When I cast her adrift, she foundered; the sea,
Overwhelmed *Maria Teresa*.
Attached by the rope, I'm quite sure you'll agree,
My ship would have sunk, not to mention poor me!
Is a cat worth more than a useful Yankee?'
The master of *Vulcan* preferred to be free
Of the Flag-Cat, *Maria Teresa*!

He was utterly wrong, for the ship did not sink;
I took charge of *Maria Teresa*.
I remained on the bridge; I slept not a wink;
I longed for some milk, even water, to drink;
While reefs by the score I just managed to jink.
I deserved a medal from Congress, I think,
As Captain, *Maria Teresa*.

I hoped against hope that quite soon I would reach
In the flagship *Maria Teresa*
An isle where the vessel could run up the beach.
The master of *Vulcan* I then would impeach;
To leave a ship drifting deprives one of speech!
So I stayed in my ship and stuck like a leech,
And skippered *Maria Teresa*.

The rest of the story is very soon told.
The flagship *Maria Teresa*
Ran ashore on an isle. I got a foothold,
Made friends with the Chief, for it pays to be bold,
And courted his daughter, the fair Marigold.
The isle is 'Cat Island', where warships have coaled.
Thus I left the *Maria Teresa*.

The captain of *Vulcan* did not get off free
For deserting *Maria Teresa*,
Since Hobson made *Vulcan* search weather and lee.
A freighter had noticed my vessel and me.
And when on Cat Island he found me, what glee!
Though he had to pay Marigold quite a large fee
For the Cat of *Maria Teresa*.

The cats of the Oceana

This *Oceana* is a stately big ship, luxuriously appointed. . . . Three big
cats – very friendly loafers; they wander all over the ship; the white one
follows the chief steward around like a dog. There is also a basket of
kittens. One of these cats goes ashore, in port, in England, Australia and
India, to see how his various families are getting along, and is seen no
more till the ship is ready to sail. No one knows how he finds out the
sailing date, but no doubt he comes down to the dock every day and takes
a look, and when he sees baggage and passengers flocking in, recognizes
that it is time to get aboard. This is what the sailors believe. . . .

from *More Tramps Abroad* by Mark Twain

Come, lovely puss

Come, lovely puss, upon my breast recline;
Do not unsheathe your claws for me to feel
But let me drown within your eyes so fine,
Compounded both of agate and of steel.

And when my fingers lazily caress
Your head, your back spring-loaded like a bow,
My hands so drunk with ecstasy confess
From you to me electric currents flow.

Ah, then in dreams I see my bride, whose glance
Like yours, my lovely puss, so deep and still,
Me pierces to the heart, a very lance
And stings; from head to foot a mystic thrill.
A heady perfume dangerous and rare
From her bronze body floats and scents the air.

after *Le Chat*
by Charles Pierre Baudelaire

Cat and leveret

'. . . *admorunt ubera tigres*'

We have remarked in a former letter how much incongruous animals, in a lonely state, may be attached to each other from a spirit of sociality; in this it may not be amiss to recount a different motive which has been known to create as strange a fondness.

My friend had a little helpless leveret brought to him, which the servants fed with milk in a spoon, and about the same time his cat kittened, and the young were dispatched and buried. The hare was soon lost, and supposed to be gone the way of most foundlings, – to be killed by some dog or cat. However, in about a fortnight, as the master was sitting in his garden in the dusk of the evening, he observed his cat, with tail erect, trotting towards him, and calling with little short inward notes of complacency, such as they use towards their kittens, and something gambolling after, which proved to be the leveret that the cat had supported with her milk, and continued to support with great affection.

Thus was a graminivorous animal nurtured by a carnivorous and predaceous one!

Why so cruel and sanguinary a beast as a cat, of the ferocious genus of *Felis*, the *murium leo,* as Linnaeus calls it, should be affected with any tenderness towards an animal which is its natural prey, is not so easy to determine.

This strange affection probably was occasioned by that *desiderium,* those tender maternal feelings which the loss of her kittens had awakened in her breast; and by the complacency and ease she derived to herself from the procuring her teats to be drawn, which were too much distended with milk, till, from habit, she became as much delighted with this foundling as if it had been her real offspring.

This incident is no bad solution of that strange circumstance which grave historians as well as the poets assert, of exposed children being sometimes nurtured by female wild beasts that probably had lost their young. For it is not one whit more marvellous that Romulus and Remus, in their infant state, should be nursed by a she-wolf, than that a poor little sucking leveret should be fostered and cherished by a blood-thirsty grimalkin.

'. . .   viridi foetam Mavortis in antro
Procubuisse lupam: geminos huic ubera circum

Ludere pendentes pueros, et lambere matrem
Impavidos: illam tereti cervice reflexam
Mulcere alternos, et corpora fingere lingua.'

from *The Natural History and Antiquities of Selborne* by Gilbert White
letter to the Hon. Daines Barrington, 9 May 1776

Cats and fish

Catus amat piscem sed non vult tangere flumen.
Mediaeval proverb, about A.D. 1200

The earliest English version of this is said to be:
Cat lufat visch, ac he nele feth wete.

Gilbert White wrote: There is a propensity belonging to common house cats that is very remarkable; I mean their violent fondness for fish, which appears to be their most favourite food. And yet nature in this instance seems to have planted in them an appetite that, unassisted, they know not how to gratify; for of all quadrupeds, cats are the least disposed towards water, and will not, when they can avoid it, deign to wet a foot, much less to plunge into that element.

from *Natural History of Selborne*
letter to Thomas Pennant Esq., 12 May 1770

Plymouth cat

In the Battery at Devil's Point, one of the Plymouth defence works, there lives a cat who has a very clever way of catching fish. Fishing has become a habit with her and every day she plunges into the sea, catches a fish and carries it in her mouth into the Naval Guard-room, where she puts it down. The cat who is now seven years old has always been a good mouser and no doubt her experience in hunting water-rats has taught her to be bold and dive for fish, of which, as is well known, cats are particularly fond. Water has now become as necessary to her as to a Newfoundland dog and every day she goes along the rocky shore, ready at a moment's notice to plunge into the sea to grab her prey.

report in the *Plymouth Journal*, 1828

The compleat angler

Mr Leonard, a very intelligent friend of mine, saw a cat catch a trout, by darting upon it in a deep clear water, at the mill at Weaford, near Lichfield. The cat belonged to Mr Stanley, who had often seen her catch fish in the same manner in summer, when the mill-pool was drawn so low that the fish could be seen. I have heard of other cats taking fish in shallow water, as they stood on the bank. This seems to be a natural method of taking their prey, usually lost by domestication, though they all retain a strong relish for fish.

Charles Darwin

A catt will never drowne if she sees the shore.
Francis Bacon, 1594

The pot of fat

A Cat having made acquaintance with a mouse, professed such great love and friendship for her, that the mouse at last agreed that they should live and keep house together.

'We must make provision for the winter,' said the cat, 'or we shall suffer hunger, and you, little mouse, must not stir out, or you will be caught in a trap.'

So they took counsel together and bought a little pot of fat. And then they could not tell where to put it for safety, but after long consideration the cat said there could not be a better place than the church, for nobody would steal there; and they would put it under the altar and not touch it until they were really in want. So this was done, and the little pot placed in safety.

But before long the cat was seized with a great wish to taste it.

'Listen to me, little mouse,' said he; 'I have been asked by my cousin to stand god-father to a little son she has brought into the world; he is white with brown spots; and they want to have the christening to-day, so let me go to it, and you stay at home and keep house.'

'Oh yes, certainly,' answered the mouse, 'pray go by all means; and when you are feasting on all the good things, think of me; I should so like a drop of the sweet red wine.'

But there was not a word of truth in all this; the cat had no cousin, and had not been asked to stand god-father: he went to the church, straight up to the little pot, and licked the fat off the top; then he took a walk over the roofs of the town, saw his acquaintances, stretched himself in the sun, and licked his whiskers as often as he thought of the little pot of fat; and then when it was evening he went home.

'Here you are at last,' said the mouse; 'I expect you have had a merry time.'

'Oh, pretty well,' answered the cat.

'And what name did you give the child?' asked the mouse.

'Top-off,' answered the cat, drily.

'Top-off!' cried the mouse, 'that is a singular and wonderful name! Is it common in your family?'

'What does it matter?' said the cat; 'it's not any worse than Crumb-picker, like your god-child.'

A little time after this the cat was again seized with a longing.

'Again I must ask you,' said he to the mouse, 'to do me a favour, and keep house alone for a day. I have been asked a second time to stand god-

82. Cat in bowenite by Fabergé

83. Cat by Whieldon

84. Three Staffordshire cats

85. Agate-ware cats

86. Two Lambeth Delft cat jugs (p. 35)

87. Sussex Cat

88. Persian bottle in shape of cat

father; and as the little one has a white ring round its neck, I cannot well refuse.'

So the kind little mouse consented, and the cat crept along by the town wall until he reached the church, and going straight to the little pot of fat, devoured half of it.

'Nothing tastes so well as what one keeps to oneself,' said he, feeling quite content with his day's work. When he reached home, the mouse asked what name had been given to the child.

'Half-gone,' answered the cat.

'Half-gone!' cried the mouse, 'I never heard such a name in my life! I'll bet it's not to be found in the calendar.'

Soon after that the cat's mouth began to water again for the fat.

'Good things always come in threes,' said he to the mouse; 'again I have been asked to stand god-father; the little one is quite black with white feet, and not any white hair on its body; such a thing does not happen every day, so you will let me go, won't you?'

'Top-off, Half-gone,' murmured the mouse, 'they are such curious names, I cannot but wonder at them!'

'That's because you are always sitting at home,' said the cat, 'in your little grey frock and hairy tail, never seeing the world, and fancying all sorts of things.'

So the little mouse cleaned up the house and set it all in order. Meanwhile the greedy cat went and made an end of the little pot of fat.

'Now all is finished one's mind will be easy,' said he, and came home in the evening, quite sleek and comfortable. The mouse asked at once what name had been given to the third child.

'It won't please you any better than the others,' answered the cat. 'It is called All-gone.'

'All-gone!' cried the mouse. 'What an unheard-of name! I never met with anything like it! All-gone! Whatever can it mean?' And shaking her head, she curled herself round and went to sleep. After that the cat was not again asked to stand god-father.

When the winter had come and there was nothing more to be had out of doors, the mouse began to think of their store.

'Come, cat,' said she, 'we will fetch our pot of fat; how good it will taste, to be sure!'

'Of course it will,' said the cat, 'just as good as if you stuck your tongue out of the window!'

So they set out, and when they reached the place, they found the pot, but it was standing empty.

'Oh, now I know what it all meant,' cried the mouse, 'now I see what sort of a partner you have been! Instead of standing god-father you have devoured it all up; first Top-off, then Half-gone, then——'

'Will you hold your tongue!' screamed the cat, 'another word, and I devour you too!'

And the poor little mouse, having 'All-gone' on her tongue, out it came, and the cat leaped upon her and made an end of her. And that is the way of the world.

from *Household Stories* by the brothers Grimm

The prophet's cat

One would hardly believe there are endowments settled in form by will, for maintaining a certain number of dogs and cats so many days in the week; yet this is commonly done; and there are people paid at Constantinople, to see the donor's intention executed, in feeding them in the streets. The butchers and bakers often set aside a small portion to bestow upon these animals. Yet with all their charity the Turks hate dogs, and never suffer them in their houses; and in a time of pestilence they kill as many as they find, thinking these unclean creatures infect the air.

On the contrary they love cats very well; whether it be for their natural cleanliness or because they sympathize with themselves in gravity; whereas the dogs are wanton, sporting and noisy. Besides, the Turks believe from I know not what tradition, that Mahomet had such a love for his cat, that, being consulted one day about a point of religion, he chose rather to cut off the skirt of his garment upon which the cat lay asleep, than to wake her in getting up, to go and speak with the person who was waiting. The Levant cats however are not more beautiful than ours, and the fine cats of a tabby-grey colour, are very scarce there; they bring them from the island of Malta, where the breed is common enough.

from *A Voyage into the Levant* by M. Tournefort, of the Royal Academy of Sciences, Chief Botanist to the King of France, etc., tr. John Ozell, 1741

According to a Hadis (i.e. a revelation from God) of Abu Qutadah, who was one of 'The Companions', Mahomet said – 'Cats are not impure; they keep watch around us'. He used water from which a cat had drunk for his purifications, and his wife Ayisha ate from a vessel from which a cat had eaten.

Mishkat. Book III

Tale of a holy cat

To Turks dogs are unclean, but cats are in an altogether different category; they are welcome in the house and none of their multitudinous offspring is ever put down. The towns therefore swarm with cats of all sizes, breeds and descriptions, most of them wild and scratching a living from whatever they can find in rubbish heaps and dustbins.

Perhaps Fatty began life as one of these. A tabby, full grown, handsome and obese, we found him one day asleep on our sofa. He was no stray, but evidently preferred our dwelling to his own. In exchange for milk and meat he relentlessly drove away other foraging cats and even attacked the occasional wandering dog.

Ali, our servant, swore he was a holy cat for, lightly impressed on the fur between his ears, were four dark parallel marks.

'You see those marks?' asked Ali. 'One day when the Prophet was saying his prayers, he was disturbed by a mouse playing impiously in front of him. Suddenly a cat removed the mouse. The Prophet was so pleased that he stroked the cat between the ears and his finger-marks never faded. So now we call any cat with those marks a holy cat.'

But Fatty seemed unconscious of his holiness and lived only for eating, sleeping and fighting. One day two Turkish friends came to lunch and saw Fatty asleep as usual.

'Ah! A holy cat,' pronounced General Hamdi Siperci, tickling Fatty's head.

'My pasha,' said Nilufer, his gentle wife, 'he is also, I'm sure, a wishing cat. He's very like the cat which Jale Hanim borrowed. Remember?'

We didn't know Jale Hanim, but she had apparently borrowed a similar cat for some curious purpose. We then learnt that any cat could be a wishing cat, but that a holy wishing cat had more appeal than an ordinary one. You had to borrow the cat, tell it in deepest confidence your wish and then set food before it. If it ate the food your chances of the wish being fulfilled depended upon whether it was a wishing cat or not, for if nothing came of your wish the animal simply could not be a wishing cat. But if your wish came true . . . !

Next morning Nilufer shyly brought a basket and borrowed Fatty. He was back before nightfall, looking inordinately smug. We suspected that Nilufer had confided some wish to him but we knew no more, for had she told us about it she would have jeopardized its fulfilment.

About a month later the general was posted to command a division in faraway eastern Turkey and, whereas he seemed pleased, Nilufer was bitterly disappointed.

Six months later they were unexpectedly back in our house. No sooner had Nilufer sat down than Fatty appeared and contentedly rubbed himself against her ankles.

'You really are a great fraud!' said Nilufer suddenly.

'Do you mean me?' I asked, astonished.

'No, not you! Fatty, of course. Fatty! a good name for a glutton. You remember I borrowed him? I told him I wished my pasha would be posted to Istanbul. In the 20 years I have been his wife he has never been stationed there. When we went to that snowbound place in the east I'm sure my pasha thought I had wished that posting to Fatty, though why he should think I wanted him sent there I don't know! And I couldn't tell him anything or my wish would have failed. Still, he was happy commanding his division, until one day he told me he had something wrong with one lung. So we were sent back here, where he has some administrative job until he has to retire next year.'

We made the usual sympathetic remarks and led the conversation to other topics. But I had the unpleasant feeling at the back of my mind that playing with wishes may be equivalent to playing with fire. I couldn't see – nor do I admit now – that Fatty could have had any influence upon the general's lung. But I knew that when he retired he would do so to Istanbul.

Meanwhile the discredited Fatty, feeling himself *de trop*, yawned and went out to the garden to sleep in the sun.

from *The Times*, 27 April 1963

The enigmatic cat

How knoweth he [man] by the vertue of his understanding the inward and secret motions of beasts? By what comparison from them to us doth he conclude the brutishnesse he ascribeth unto them? When I am playing with my cat, who knowes whether she have more sport in dallying with me, than I have in gaming with her? We entertaine one another with mutuall apish trickes. If I have my houre to begin or to refuse, so hath she hers.

from the essay on Raymond Sebond
by M. E. de Montaigne, tr. by John Florio, 1603

Cats are a mysterious kind of folk. There is more passing in their minds than we are aware of.

Sir Walter Scott

Touch not the cat

And because of their fear of such a punishment any who have caught sight of one of these animals [cats] lying dead withdraw to a great distance and shout with lamentations and protestations that they found the animal already dead. So deeply implanted also in the heart of the common people is their superstitious regard for these animals and so unalterable are the emotions cherished by every man regarding the honour due to them that once, at the time when Ptolemy their king had not as yet been given by the Romans the appelation of 'friend' and the people were exercising all zeal in courting the favour of the embassy from Italy which was then visiting Egypt and, in their fear, were intent upon giving no cause for complaint or war, when one of the Romans killed a cat and the multitude rushed in a crowd to his house, neither the officials sent by the king to beg the man off nor the fear of Rome which all the people felt were enough to save the man from punishment, even though his act had been an accident. And this incident we relate, not from hearsay, but we saw it with our own eyes on the occasion of the visit we made to Egypt.

from *Bibliotheca Historica* (*c.* 50 B.C.) by Diodorus Siculus tr. by C. H. Oldfather

Suttee of the cats

The number of domestic animals in Egypt is very great, and would be still greater were it not for what befalls the cats. As the females, when they have kittened, no longer seek the company of the males, these last, to obtain once more their companionship, practise a curious artifice. They seize the kittens, carry them off, and kill them, but do not eat them afterwards. Upon this the females, being deprived of their young, and longing to supply their place, seek the males once more, since they are particularly fond of their offspring. On every occasion of a fire in Egypt the strangest prodigy occurs with the cats. The inhabitants allow the fire to rage as it pleases, while they stand about at intervals and watch these animals which, slipping by the men or else leaping over them, rush headlong into the flames. When this happens, the Egyptians are in deep affliction. If a cat dies in a private house by a natural death, all the inmates of the house shave their eyebrows. . . . The cats on their decease are taken to the city of Bubastis, where they are embalmed, after which they are buried in certain sacred repositories.

from the Second Book of the History of Herodotus, entitled *Euterpe*
tr. by George Rawlinson

The Feast of St John

It is recounted by Sir James Frazer in *The Golden Bough* that in the fires which used to be kindled in the Place de Grève in Paris in midsummer, it was the custom to burn a barrel, basket, or sack full of live cats. The sack was hung from a tall pole in the middle of the bonfire. The people would take home the embers and ashes from the fire, in the belief that they brought them good luck. The king himself often watched the fire, some-times even lighting it himself. Louis XIV was the last king to take part in this horrible ceremony, in 1648. It is reported that the Dauphin who became Louis XIII induced his father, Henry IV, to reprieve the cats on one occasion, so that they were not sent to the '*bûcher* [pile of faggots] *de la St Jean*'. The celebration used to take place on the Festival of St John.

Similar practices existed in Luxembourg and in Metz, where 13 cats used to be burned alive in a wooden cage on 24 June, the eve of St John's festival. It is good to hear that the Marshal (or his lady) of Armentières stopped the use of cats in the late eighteenth century (1773 or 1777). At Store Magleby near Copenhagen, a live cat used to be imprisoned in a cask at which horsemen used to tilt, on the eve of Shrove Tuesday. At Ypres an annual festival on the second Sunday in May commemorates, among other cat legends, the mediaeval custom of throwing two or three cats from the famous belfry. In each case, the cats symbolized evil, of which the people were ridding themselves.

On a cat, ageing

He blinks upon the hearth-rug,
And yawns in deep content,
Accepting all the comforts
That Providence has sent.

Louder he purrs, and louder,
In one glad hymn of praise
For all the night's adventures,
For quiet, restful days.

Life will go on for ever,
With all that cat can wish:
Warmth and the glad procession
Of fish and milk and fish.

Only – the thought disturbs him –
He's noticed once or twice,
The times are somehow breeding
A nimbler race of mice.

Alexander Gray

Dedication

Dear Furry Shade! in regions of the Dead,
On pleasant plains, by murmurous waters, led;
What placid joys your brindled bosom swell!
While smiling virgins crowned with asphodel
Bring brimming bowls of milk in sacrifice,
And, passing plump and sleek, th'Elysian mice
Sport round your feet, and frisk, and glide away,
Captured at last – a not too facile prey.
Yet, with each earthly care and tremor stilled,
With every wish of cat-hood well fulfilled,
Still sometimes turn, with retrospective gaze,
To count the sweets of less luxurious days,
When you were wont to take your simple ease
Couched at my feet or stretched along my knees:
When never cloud our loving-kindness knew,
(Though now and then, alas! I punished you),
Still were you fain, conciliating, bland,
With velvet cheek to chafe th' avenging hand.
Still would you watch, did I but chance to roam,
Supine upon the threshold of our home
Until, my brief-paced aberrations o'er,
With purrings deep you welcomed me once more.
O dearly-loved! Untimely lost! – to-day
An offering at your phantom feet I lay:
Purr fond applause, and take in gracious kind
This little wreath of various verses twined;
Nor, though Persephone's own Puss you be,
Let Orcus breed oblivion – of me.

Graham R. Tomson

Two epitaphs

Puss passer-by, within this simple tomb
   Lies one whose life fell Atropos hath shred;
The happiest cat on earth hath heard her doom,
   And sleeps for ever in a marble bed.
Alas! what long delicious days I've seen!
   O cats of Egypt, my illustrious sires,
You who on altars, bound with garlands green,
   Have melted hearts, and kindled fond desires;
Hymns in your praise were paid, and offerings too,
   But I'm not jealous of those rites divine,
Since Ludovisa loved me, close and true,
   Your ancient glory was less proud than mine.
To live, a simple pussy, by her side
Was nobler far than to be deified.

La Mothe le Vayer on the favourite cat of the Duchess of Maine
tr. by Edmund Gosse

Worn out with age and dire disease, a cat,
Friendly to all save wicked mouse and rat,
I'm sent at last to ford the Stygian lake,
And to the infernal coast a voyage make.
Me Proserpine received, and smiling said:
'Be blessed within these mansions of the dead.
Enjoy among thy velvet-footed loves,
Elysium's sunny banks, and shady groves!'
'But if I've well deserved (O gracious Queen),
If patient under sufferings I have been,
Grant me at least one night to visit home again,
Once more to see my home and mistress dear,
And purr these grateful accents in her ear:
"Thy faithful cat, thy poor departed slave,
Still loves her mistress, e'en beyond the grave." '

Imitated in English from the Latin of Dr Jortin (see p. 199)

Last words to a dumb friend

Pet was never mourned as you,
Purrer of the spotless hue,
Plumy tail and wistful gaze,
While you humoured our queer ways,
Or outshrilled your morning call
Up the stairs and through the hall –
Foot suspended in its fall –
While, expectant, you would stand
Arched, to meet the stroking hand;
Till your way you chose to wend
Yonder, to your tragic end.

Never another pet for me!
Let your place all vacant be;
Better blankness day by day
Than companion torn away.
Better bid his memory fade,
Better blot each mark he made,
Selfishly escape distress
By contrived forgetfulness,
Than preserve his prints to make
Every morn and eve an ache.

From the chair whereon he sat
Sweep his fur, nor wince thereat;
Rake his little pathways out
Mid the bushes round about;
Smooth away his talons' mark
From the claw-worn pine-tree bark,
Where he climbed as dusk enbrowned
Waiting us who loitered round.

Strange it is this speechless thing,
Subject to our mastering,
Subject for his life and food
To our gift, and time, and mood;
Timid pensioner of us Powers,
His existence ruled by ours,

Should – by crossing at a breath
Into safe and shielded death,
By the merely taking hence
Of his insignificance –
Loom as largened to the sense,
Shape as part, above man's will,
Of the Imperturbable.

As a prisoner, flight debarred,
Exercising in a yard,
Still retain I, troubled, shaken,
Mean estate, by him forsaken;
And this home, which scarcely took
Impress from his little look,
By his faring to the Dim,
Grows all eloquent of him.

Housemate, I can think you still
Bounding to the window-sill,
Over which I vaguely see
Your small mound beneath the tree,
Showing in the autumn shade
That you moulder where you played.

Thomas Hardy

Epitaphium felis

Most books about cats are meant by their authors as tributes to their own much loved cats, whose short lives and blithe spirits they cannot bear to be forgotten. These last pages have contained a few of the more moving of such tributes. It is fitting that the symposium should conclude with the Latin epitaph on his cat Felis by Dr Jortin, Archdeacon of London, who himself died in 1770. Like another eminent St Paul's divine, also a scholar, writing in the twentieth century on the death of a daughter in childhood, Dr Jortin felt that what he had to say could only be said in Latin – that to express his deep love for his cat without being guilty of the sin of 'inordinate affection', Latin alone would serve.

Decessit Felis Anno MDCCLVII, vixit annos XIV, menses XI, dies IV

Fessa annis, morboque gravi, mitissima Felis,
    infernos tandem cogor adire lacus:
et mihi subridens Proserpina dixit, 'Habeto
    Elysios soles, Elysiumque nemus.'
Sed, bene simerui, facilis Regina Silentium,
    Da mihi saltem una nocte redire domum;
nocte redire domum, dominoque haec dicere in aurem,
    'Te tua fida etiam trans Stygia Felis amat.'

Bibliography

Aberconway, Christabel Lady: *A Dictionary of Cat Lovers*, Michael Joseph, 1949
Anderson, M. D.: *Animal Carvings in British Churches*, Cambridge, 1938
Baring-Gould, S.: *Lives of the British Saints*, Cymmrodorian Society, 1907–1913
Bond, F.: *Wood Carvings in English Churches: I Misericords*, Humphrey Milford, 1910
Brewer, Ebeneezer Cobham: *A Dictionary of Phrase and Fable*, Cassell
Butler, Alban: *Lives of the Saints*, Burns Oates & Co., 1926–1938
Collins, Arthur Henry: *Symbolism of Animals and Birds represented in English Church Architecture*, Sir I. Pitman & Sons, 1913
Conan-Fallex, Jacqueline: *Le Chat dans la Littérature et dans l'Art*, Les Éditions des 'Meilleurs Livres', 1926
Cox, J. Charles: *Bench-ends in English Churches*, Humphrey Milford, 1916
Dale-Green, Patricia: *Cult of the Cat*, Heinemann, 1963
Drake, Maurice & Wilfred: *Saints and their Emblems*, T. Werner Laurie, 1916
Druce, G. C.: *Animals in English Woodcarvings*, Walpole Soc. III
Edmunds, William H.: *Pointers and Clues to the subjects of Chinese and Japanese Art*, Sampson Low & Co., 1934
Evans, E. P.: *Animal Symbolism in Ecclesiastical Architecture*, Heinemann, 1896
Ferguson, George W.: *Signs and Symbols in Christian Art*, Oxford, 1954
Frazer, J. G.: *The Golden Bough: a study in magic and religion*, Macmillan, 1900
Halliwell, T. O.: *Nursery Rhymes of England* (2nd edition), London, 1843
Joseph, Michael: *Cat's Company*, Michael Joseph, 1946
Ker, John Bellenden: *Popular English Phrases and Nursery Rhymes*, 1837
Larwood, Jacob, and Hotten, John Camden: *History of Signboards*, Chatto & Windus, 1866 (7th edition), and (revised ed.) *English Inn Signs*, 1951
Lawrence, A. W.: *Classical Sculpture. Its History from the Earliest Times to the death of Constantine*, Jonathan Cape, 1929
Mee, Arthur: Ed. of *King's England* series of County guides, Hodder & Stoughton, 1930 onwards
Oldfield, H. M.: *The Cat in the Mysteries of Religion and Magic*, Rider, 1930(31)
Opie, Iona and Peter (Ed.): *Oxford Dictionary of Nursery Rhymes*, Clarendon Press, 1951(52)
Panofsky, Professor Erwin: *The Life and Art of Albrecht Dürer* (4th edition), Princeton University Press, 1955
Phipson, Emma: *Choir stalls and their carvings*, Batsford, 1896
Rappoport, Angelo S.: *Myth and Legend in Ancient Israel*, Gresham Pub. Co., 1928
Robinson, B. W.: *Kuniyoshi*, H.M.S.O., 1961
Roeder, Helen: *Saints and their Attributes, with a guide to locations and patronage*, Longmans, Green & Co., London, 1955
Stevenson, Burton: *Book of Proverbs, Maxims and Familiar Phrases*, Routledge & Kegan Paul, 1949
Stuart, Dorothy Margaret: *A Book of Cats, Literary, Legendary and Historical*, Methuen, 1959
Surtees, Robert Smith: *Handley Cross*, Simpkin, Marshall & Co., London, 1891
Wildridge, T. Tindall: *The Grotesque in Church Art*, William Andrews, 1899
Wright, J.: *The English Dialect Dictionary*, Frowde, 1898–1905

Index

Figures in italics refer to plates; illustrations in the text are preceded by *page*